Escape to Paradise

Adventures and Misadventures around the Romantic Caribbean Sea

Paul Franson

© Copyright 2014 by Paul Franson. All rights reserved.

Manufactured in the United States.

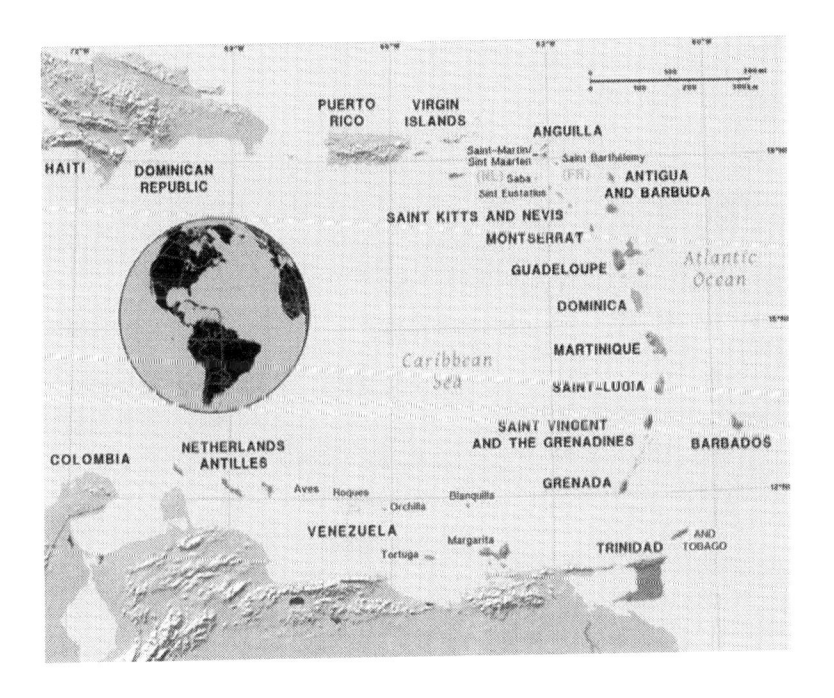

The eastern Caribbean Sea

My Escapes to Paradise

I've had the distinct pleasure – though it didn't always seem that way at the time – of spending quite a bit of time in the most exciting place on earth, the Caribbean Sea.

Variously called the Lesser Antilles, the West Indies or just the Caribbean, the small islands between the rough Atlantic Ocean and the calm Caribbean Sea are unique. Once the sources of some of the greatest if immoral wealth on earth, they inspired great battles among European powers who sought to possess them.

Then they lost that position, and slid into the background until today's tourism has once more made them treasured designations.

I've been there in charters in small sailboats, visits to many islands by airplane, four cruises on large sailing ships, and most significantly, living on my own sailboat there for a couple of years.

This book is a recounting of those times, some in more depth than others, with the greatest space naturally dedicated to my life on my boat in Antigua.

I've also thrown in a section on the fascinating food of the islands, based mostly but not exclusively on the time I spent in Antigua.

I hope my adventures and misadventures provide armchair travelers – and those who hope to visit – some pleasure and some insight.

Do expect inconsistencies and redundancies, however, for these pieces were written over many years and for different purposes. And many things have likely changed since then.

Paul Franson
Napa Valley 2014

Escape to Paradise

The eastern Caribbean Sea	3
Forward: My Escapes to Paradise	4
The Background	6
The British Virgin Islands	7
Visiting Puerto Rico	13
A trip to Hedonism	28
Sailing aboard the Mandalay	31
Sailing alone on the Star Clipper	38
Escape to Paradise?	40
From my Time on Antigua	94
Report from Antigua Classic Yacht Regatta	102
Antigua Sailing Week	105
Sailing in the Grenadines	107
A Return to Paradise	113
A Guide to Cruising in the Grenadines	123
A Visit to a Forgotten Part of the Caribbean	129
The Caribbean Cuisine	138

The Background

Even when I was a boy, I was fascinated with the Caribbean. I read books about the exotic area, even preparing a report on its history when I was in junior high school.

This was before the islands of the Lesser Antilles gained independence, and I read about them and fantasized over the picture books I found of living and sailing there.

I read *Our Virgin Island*, the tale of a couple's life on a deserved island in the British Virgin Island just before World War II, and James Michener's *Caribbean* and Herman Wouk's *Don't Stop the Carnival*. All had a lasting impression.

I was intrigued by these historic islands, each so close yet having a different character: English colonies, Dutch Colonies, French departments, former Danish, Swedish and Spanish colonies and American territories.

Some are high islands with extinct volcanoes (or even a live one in Montserrat); some are low. Some are sophisticated, some fairly primitive. Some court tourists, while others mostly live on agriculture or fishing.

I can't imagine any places more beautiful, and the ability to sail a few miles and be in a completely different – and always fascinating – environment is unique anywhere in the world.

So the rest of this book is a reflection of my love of the Caribbean and my visits there.

I should mention that English-speaking people living there pronounce it car i BÉ an, not ca RÍB ean.

The British Virgin Islands

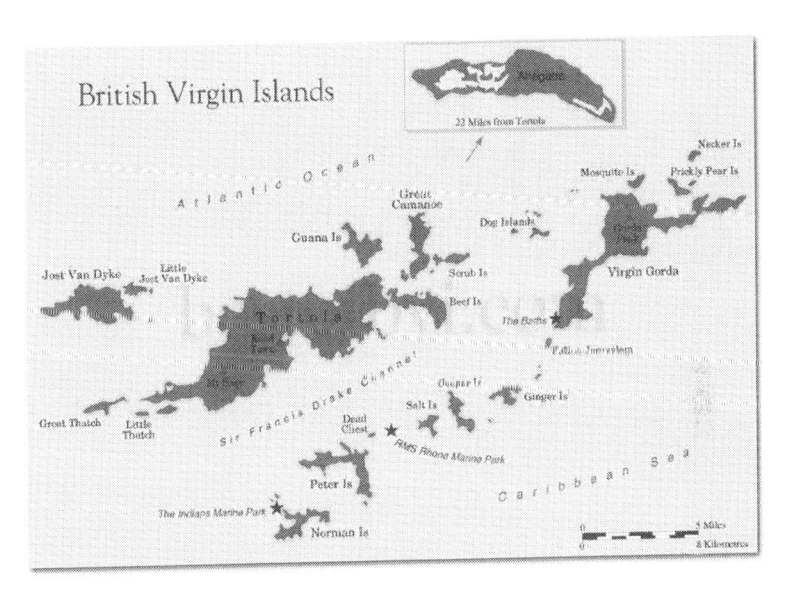

I made my first visit to the Caribbean in the early '70s, when my former, and now late, wife Teddy and I lived in Manhattan Beach in California.

We had a modest 24-ft. sailboat, one of the many boats called Islander by a variety of manufacturers. We often sailed it to Catalina island 26 miles across the sea, as the song goes, enjoying the almost tropical ambience of its harbors and coves. Those adventures could be a story in itself.

We were members of a modest local yacht club better known for its parties than its sailing. It was then called the Palos Verdes Yacht Club, but later renamed itself to reflect its location in Redondo Beach harbor.

We thoroughly enjoyed our trips to Catalina, but jumped at the chance when the club organized a trip to sail in the British Virgin Islands, unquestionably the best place in the world for virgin charterers to head.

They organized three boats worth, each with half a dozen people. Our boat had three men and three women, among them people owning four boats and reasonably competent sailors (Okay, all were more experienced than Teddy and I were). Other than Teddy and me, they were all single.

We embarked on the long flights – most west coasters don't realize that the prime islands of the Caribbean are east of the east coast of the United States, and lie in the Atlantic time zone, four times zones distant.

After a stop in Miami, we ended up in San Juan, where, exhausted, we boarded the DC-3's left over from World War II to fly to Tortola in the British Islands.

I most remember seeing the liquid leaking out of the two engines. I worriedly told the stewardess, as they were called then, and she said that was normal. We should worry if the dripping stops, for the engine leaked oil as part of its lubrication.

Soon we were flying over the fabled island and landed at the modest airport on its eastern end. The airport was a landing strip and a small cement block hut.

We got off and experienced the Caribbean.

You can never forget the combination of heavy hot air and smells of burning trash and fragrant tropical flowers mixed with the breezes from the sea.

Soon, we were transported to a modest motel in Road Town by the harbor where the Moorings had its base; we had wisely come a day early to acclimatize.

We also bought supplies. We had made a list, and bought the provisions at a nearby supermarket well accustomed to novice charterers.

We bought a lot of beer, some of the modest wine, and lots of other food. The meat was frozen, and the boat we chartered had a freezer.

I don't remember that evening beyond eating dinner, but soon was asleep.

The next morning, we boarded the 40-ft monohull – catamarans were almost unknown then – loaded our modest baggage aboard with the food and beverages, and set off.

The British Virgin Islands – they're one of the few British colonies still in the empire – are ideal for sailing. Set more or less south west to northeast, they're mostly protected from the heaviest winds of the Caribbean, providing a fairly narrow channel separating two rows of small islands.

We headed for Norman Island for our first night, a short trip giving us a chance to get comfortable with the boat.

Like some of the other islands, Norman Island, the reputed inspiration for *Treasure Island,* is privately owned and we couldn't go ashore, but we tucked into a cozy cove, set the anchor and set about relaxing, swimming in the warm waters, sunbathing and drinking beer and wine.

As the sun set – as it does about 6 p.m. year round in the tropics, we drank some cheap sparkling wine to celebrate, then started dinner.

The boat came with a neat barbeque that was fastened to its aft – that's the back of the boat if you don't understand salty talk – rail, hanging over the water so you could safely dump the hot coats into the water. Fiberglass boats, as this was, are held together by an inflammable resin, after all.

We had some beautiful – and expensive – steaks for our first night, but at some point, someone accidentally loosened the BBQ, and dumped both the coals and the steaks in the deep.

The fish ate well that night. We didn't.

The next few days, we sailed among the islands, stopping to snorkel over the famed wreck of the Rhone – best known as the site for Jacqueline Bisset's T shirt sequences in *The Deep*, which was filmed there.

We went ashore where we could, but soon ended up at a relatively civilized island, Virgin Gorda. Our captain for the day, who owned a 48-ft. boat and had sailed all over, almost knocked down the dock on the way in.

We eventually went ashore, explored the famed Baths, weird rock formations half in the water where we splashed around and watched a few exhibitionistic couples playing around.

Afterwards, we enjoyed some great ice cream.

It was here that we noticed that the freezer, and in fact the refrigerator wasn't cooling. We got on the radio, and the charter company said that it didn't know about that, but it headed our way with big blocks of ice and did so every few days for the rest of the voyage.

We then sailed around to the far end of Virgin Gorda to the reef-locked harbor at the Bitter End Yacht Club. There we spent the night, enjoying the companionship of the restaurant and club.

It was about here that one of the other boats offered to trade one of its crew with one of ours "for variety."

We suspected a rat and demurred, and they soon collected funds to sent the obnoxious member home early.

We, by contrast, could not have had a better crew. Everyone got along well, and no one felt the need to be the boss all the time.

From Virgin Gorda, we sailed the long way (maybe 20 miles) to Tortola's West End for more shore partying, then around the island to Cane Garden Bay. Here as at many other places, there was no dock. We dinghied ashore, getting a bit wet in the warm Caribbean waters in the process.

Then we stopped at Sandy Cay, everyone's vision of a tropical island with palm trees and sparkling beaches. We explored the tiny island, but I'm sorry to say we didn't find any buried treasure.

Soon we headed for Jost Van Dyke, party central in the BVI.

Most people head for the Great Harbor, where Foxy's bar has become legendary.

We, however, sailed to Little Harbor to the east to have dinner at Sidney's Peace and Love. We anchored in the bar and gave our orders over the radio: five lobsters, one chicken.

About an hour later, a power boar came rushing into the bay, apparently delivering our lobsters to the modest restaurant.

Come sundown, we piled into the dinghy and headed ashore. The proprietor explained that drinks were on the honor system, and we started digging into the beer, rum and half gallons of Gallo wine.

After enjoying the excellently prepared dinner, we continued to party, noticing that all the staff had left.

Most of us found T shirts as souvenirs; for years, I was amazed to find how many people had been there when I wore my shirt from Sidney's Peace and Love.

According to what I see, it's still going strong.

By then, we sensed that the wonderful holiday was drawing to a close. We sailed around the back (north) side of Tortola and anchored near the aforementioned Virgin Island, Marina Cay, now known as Bellamy Cay.

I had to leave then for some commitments in California, but the rest of the crew sailed around to Road Town to complete their voyage.

It was one of the best vacations I've ever had.

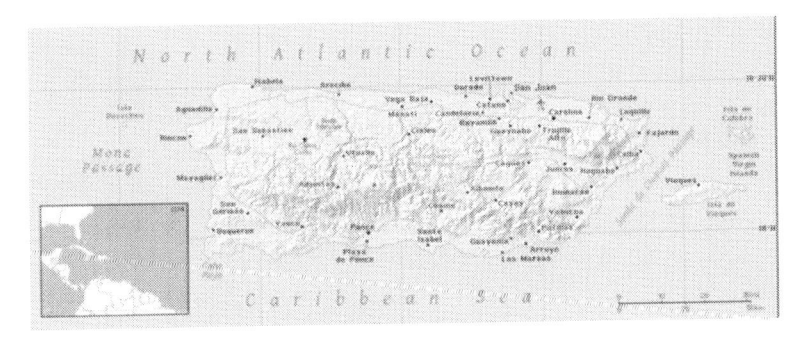

Visiting Puerto Rico

My next trips to the Caribbean were as the editor of *Electronic Business* magazine, a magazine for executives and managers of high-tech companies.

In those days, tax incentives were offered for American companies to establish plants in this American colony, er, territory. It was quite popular with both electronic and pharmaceutical companies, and they provide much employment.

I was invited to visit in the hopes that I would write favorably about the island as a location for assembly plants.

I had a great time, visiting twice and seeing much of the island and getting a chance to explore not only historic San Juan but the mountainous and southern coast.

There I developed an increased appreciation for the food, which is similar to Cuban food.

Later I returned for, of all things, a wine festival and stayed in the picturesque Old Town.

One of my revelations there was visiting the Bacardí rum distillery. I've been to more wineries than I care to think about, many breweries and a few artisan stills, but nothing prepared me for this huge plant.

The Bacardí family was one in Cuba, but Castro expropriated their property and they moved operations to Puerto Rico.

There they built a modern factory to make rum. Their costs intrigued me after covering the wine business, where land for grapes in places like Napa Valley is so expensive, and winemaking takes a lot of expensive capital equipment that's really only used for a month or so.

By contrast, most rum is made from a waste product from refining sugar (molasses) and the nutritious waste from the process is sold for animal feed. They can brew the base material year round, so have very efficient use of equipment. They even sell the carbon dioxide generated to the neighboring Coca Cola plant!

I should point out that some rums available in Puerto Rico aren't sold here. I'm told some are some of the best, but didn't get a chance to confirm that and wouldn't know anyway if I tasted them. I'm not a rum drinker.

Needless to say, the beaches in much of Puerto Rico are beautiful and the climate is almost perfect except for an occasional hurricane. Though Spanish is the primary language, anyone who deals with tourists probably speaks English well.

I later visited Puerto Rico a number of times, some long layovers when flying farther southeast, another for a food and wine festival; who'd ever think they'd have a wine festival there, where rum and beer are the most popular drinks!

For most West Coasters who've visited the Caribbean, Puerto Rico is the place you change planes to get almost anywhere else. In doing so, they've missed a tropical paradise that is becoming a prime destination for travelers.

Puerto Rico has a magnificent setting.

The 100-by-35-mile island has classic beautiful beaches ringed with palm trees, a rugged mountainous heart containing a true rain forest, and history aplenty including massive stone forts and the fascinating 500-year-old walled city of San Juan.

What's attracting a new class of visitors is a fusion culture that marries the best local traditions with influences from Africa, New York, California, Asia and Europe.

Food, drink, music and dance reflect this fusion, resulting in a vibrant lifestyle that appeals particularly to Californians.

Everyone you're likely to encounter speaks English, which is required in school.

The local Spanish is shot out in machine-gun torrents, making the Mexican Spanish familiar to most San Franciscans seem leisurely in contrast.

For a start, there's Nuevo Criollo food, the new Creole cuisine based on indigenous ingredients and traditions prepared by chefs who've perfected their craft in West Coast and Asian restaurants. One example is Roberto Treviño of the trendy Parrot Club in Old San Juan, who's from Sunnyvale and worked in several San Francisco restaurants before moving to the island.

Traditional Puerto Rican cuisine combines local tropical fruits, vegetables and seafood known to the Taino (Arawak) Indians with a strong Spanish heritage all fused by African cooks.

The food features heavy stews, savory pastries and fried food, tasty but not particularly designed for today's healthy lifestyle.

New chefs have lightened the food, adding Pacific touches any San Franciscan would recognize to create a delectable cuisine that transcends traditional cooking.

Drinks, too, have changed. They still feature island rum and tropical fruit, like Daiquiris and piña coladas, but Bacardi, the huge rum maker that moved to its Puerto Rico distillery when Castro confiscated its plant in Cuba, now makes rums to suit almost any taste.

It's in partying, however, where Californians could learn a few things from young Puerto Ricans.

They love to dress up and go out late in the evening, often hitting clubs with driving hot, live, local music and staying until early in the morning. Bands play both fierce Afro-Latin rhythms and alternative variations, and it's impossible to sit still when their beat throbs through your body.

Fortunately, after a night on the town, visitors don't have to get up early. When they do arise, they can enjoy a breakfast of local tropical fruit and some of the world's best coffee, then lie like lazy lizards on beautiful beaches between dips in the bath-like turquoise water.

The northern coast of the island features many world-class resorts including the new Westin Rio Mar with two golf courses just east of San Juan. There's a whole resort row on the beach at Condado in town, and the resorts feature every amenity, including casinos and fine restaurants.

Some visitors stay in paradores, traditional "bed and breakfasts" scattered throughout the island, many on beaches on the southern (Caribbean) coast.

For the ultimate relaxation, there are quiet inns on Culebra and Vieques, two small islands in the "Spanish Virgins" only a few miles from the American and British Virgins east of the Puerto Rico.

Puerto Rico's heart lies in Old San Juan, a walled city that contains El Morro, a magnificent fortress that guarded the island's excellent harbor for 500 years. Many of the most interesting restaurants, shops, dubs and museums are tucked in the old town, and though some of the buildings are still being restored, the dense area is a perfect place to explore on foot; only a local would be "loco" enough to drive on its narrow streets, much less try to park.

There are two superb hotels in Old San Juan. El Convento next to the cathedral was once a nunnery but you don't have to take any vows to stay there now. The new Wyndham lies on the recently upgraded harbor within walking distance of the embarcadero that once again attracts Local families as well as visitors to its markets, music and museums.

Along with Old San Juan and the beaches, another prime attraction in Puerto Rico is the rain forest. High in the mountains, but only a short distance from San Juan, the park contains fascinating plants and animals you can enjoy from many hiking trails. You might even catch a glimpse of the rare native Puerto Rican parrot. The forest is easily accessible by tour or rental car.

Puerto Rico is a great place to visit. I'd like to return and see the "Spanish Virgin Islands" of Culebra and Vieques off its eastern coast, which have been freed from Naval control and are now once more accessible to the public. They're only a short distance from the British (and American Virgin Islands, but almost no one sails that way. It's easy to sail west, tough returning into the prevailing winds and currents.

Sailing on the Polynesia

My next adventure in the Caribbean was aboard the Polynesia, one of the late and lamented Windjammer Bareboat Cruise sailing ships.

I was single by then. I flew into Phillipsburg in Sint Maarten, the Dutch two-thirds of the island of St. Martin (The other third is French).

I came a couple of days early to explore the island and adjust to the four-hour time change. I stayed at a typical and pleasant tourist hotel on the water west of town but a fairly easy walk.

Phillipsburg is about shopping. It has restaurants and clubs, but as a tax-free port, it attracts many people out to buy electronics and other luxuries.

It's mostly one street curling around the harbor, though there is a back street mostly frequented by locals.

The first day I was there, I met a nice lady from New York staying in my hotel, and we had dinner in town. It was a tasty meal of seafood, which is what I almost always order when I'm near the sea.

Walking back from dinner on the beach, I found that the voluminous layers of cloth she was wearing hid the fact that she wasn't wearing anything else.

It is the Caribbean, after all.

The next day, as she had a car, we visited the very French village of Marigot then explored the island, grabbing lunch at one of the many small beach restaurants along the western shore. The food is mostly authentic Creole, seafood, tropical vegetables and fruit with good French wine.

Continuing clockwise around the island, we came to St. Martin's famed nude beach, Orient Beach. All I can say is that I was thinner then! I sensed that my companion was a hippie at heart, though a school teacher on Long Island.

That night, I boarded Polynesia with some regret, for she asked me to spend a last night ashore, but I was anxious to get aboard and meet my new crew members. I wish she could have joined us.

The Polynesia

The Polynesia was a 250-ft. four-masted steel schooner that carried about 110 passengers.

I had a tiny cabin as a single guy, but it was enough. The bath was a small cubicle with a shower over the head.

These ships were Animal House on the water. It was modest accommodations and food combined with non-stop partying.

The heavy Polynesia *could* sail, but the engine was usually going, too.

We first sailed from Phillipsburg for the nearby and très chic French island of St. Barts 20 miles away.

We first anchored at the almost uninhabited west end where we went ashore to enjoy the beach, then the ship moved closer to town, though not into the tiny harbor of Gustavia with its fancy boutiques and expensive restaurants. The ship was small for a cruise ship but too big for the compact harbor.

The island was once Swedish, by the way. The American Virgin Islands were Danish until we bought them during World War II to protect the Panama Canal.

Later made famous when Jimmy Buffett sang about a cheeseburger in paradise there, St. Barts is now a haven for the uber-wealthy. We saw many beautiful people, but didn't recognize any movie stars.

Nevertheless, we found an inexpensive lunch, cheeseburgers, of course.

Meals on board were basic, but most days we were in fascinating islands for lunch, then boarded and had dinner as we sailed to the next island.

The ship provided unlimited if mediocre wine with dinner.

After dinners, we played games, listened to music, danced, head stories from Captain Jock, some probably true, and drank luscious concoctions filled with cheap spirits.

Let's be honest. We partied hard. The wine was free with dinner, the booze was cheap, and the music intoxicating.

At nights as we sailed between islands, Scottish Captain Jock would finally tell us hard-core party animals to keep it down. We often slipped into rum-induced sleep on deck, awakening when the sun rose near 6 a.m., as it does year round in the tropics.

I had a great time.

I met some friendly single ladies, though none to hook up for more than a night or so, and enjoyable couples including a pair of self-described Coon-Ass Cajuns from Louisiana.

They thankfully protected me from a woman who had staked me out the first night.

The wife in one of the couples in our group was clearly unhappy in her marriage, and was seeking a tropical adventure, Her husband clearly understood. He watched her like a hawk for the whole week.

As we left port each evening, Captain Jock played Amazing Grace on the bagpipes, a sound I still recall.

Next on our tour was the rarely visited island of St. Eustatius, once the richest place on earth. It's about 30 miles from St. Barts and we passed high Dutch Saba, one of the few islands I haven't visited, on the way.

Dutch Statia, as it's called, was once the trading ground for the wealth of the Indies, but when it recognized the United States, Admiral Rodney sacked and burned it, and it never recovered. An earthquake sunk most of the port; now a few buildings line the waterfront, but most are on a cliff high above.

Now a peaceful island of 1,500 people, it has no lodgings with more than 20 rooms, and it won't allow big cruise ships to call; large ships with thousands of passengers would overwhelm the small island. The Polynesia with 110 was about right.

We did take a tour, visiting the ruins of the first synagogue in the Americas, seeing the old fort and checking out the old harbor town underwater with face masks.

Sailing south, we next stopped at St. Kitts, once called St. Christopher. A former British colony wasn't a tourist island, but primarily engaged in agriculture. It even still grows sugar cane, and an old railway used to deliver the cane serves as a tourist attraction.

It has a magnificent old fort but other than beaches, not much for tourists. The island is shaped like a cricket bat, and there's not much but beaches along the southern handle.

The next island south, Nevis, was then very old Caribbean, with no big hotels, but a Four Seasons transformed the island in the future.

Nesbit Plantation on Nevis

Alexander Hamilton was born on Nevis, and we visited his old home, but for us the big pleasure was relaxing at Nesbit Plantation, a low-key resort on the island's windy and rough east side.

I was to return there a number of times on future cruises, always enjoying the visit.

Next was Monserrat, strangely still a British colony although all its neighbors are independent nations (Nevis and St. Kitts in a shotgun marriage).

This was before its volcano erupted, and we toured the island including the volcano, and had "mountain chicken" (giant frog) in the capital of Plymouth, which has since been buried like Pompeii, though fortunately without loss of life.

It once featured an important recording studio used by many British musicians. That, like the old capital of Plymouth is now buried in ash and lava. Most of the small population has left, but it has developed a bit of a volcanic tourist appeal.

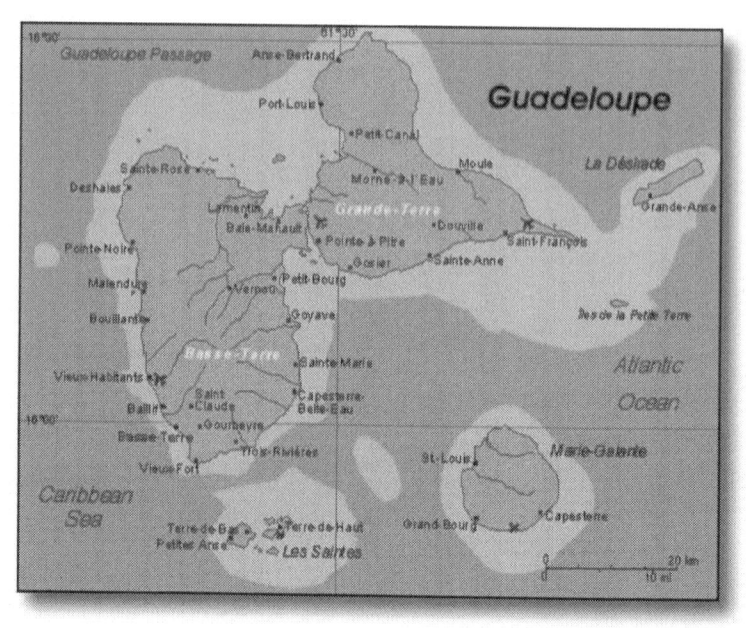

Guadeloupe was the next island. A French department or state, it's shaped like a butterfly with one mountainous and one flat wing. I've never visited the capital, Pointe a Pitre, PP on the stern of French boats.

Guadeloupe has received some recent fame, for the popular TV series, *Death in Paradise,* is filmed in the small town of Deshaies in the northwest, though it's described as the island of "Sainte Marie."

During the French revolution, a fanatic named Hugues came with a guillotine and killed all the educated people, white or black in one of the saddest tales in an area that has suffered so many.

The island still seems backward in some ways compared to Martinique, which was thankfully occupied by the British during the French revolution – one of many see see-saws of power in the West Indies – and was spared Guadeloupe's agony.

Our next stop was perhaps my favorite one. The tiny Iles des Saintes off the south coast of Guadalupe are a dependency of that French island department.

The Saints are small dry islands without enough land or water to grow sugar cane. They were one of the few islands settled by white settlers and never had many slaves.

That saved the islands from the inhumane treatment of slaves and the slave revolts that killed the owners, but had one unfortunate side affect.

The Breton and Norman fishermen were isolated and interbred. You could see the signs among some of the working white people, though the officials were sophisticated, smartly dressed, well-educated black Guadeloupeans from the "mainland."

During World War II, the islands were controlled until 1943 by Vichy French vassals of Hitler, but local people resisted and many sailed to nearby British islands to join the Free French fighting the Nazis.

After the war, supposedly the French government sent a ship filled with lusty young naval cadets to the island, and nine months later, babies with more vigorous heritage were born.

The islands are famed for a sea battle in 1782 when Admiral Rodney whipped the French fleet, an important battle in the far-off European wars.

The French fleet still kept the British fleet from reinforcing Cornwallis at Yorktown, which likely was the definitive battle of the American Revolution.

Vive la France! Otherwise, we'd be looking forward to rule by King Charles.

The town has basically one long street with casual restaurants and tourist shops. There are almost no cars or even taxis as you can walk everywhere, though scooters are popular.

25

Few things are better than a grilled lobster just out of the sea, and that's the perfect meal for a visitor to Terre de Haut, the largest and most populated island.

You certainly deserve one after climbing the hill to visit Fort Napoleon, which has been closed twice when I visited though the view was fantastic.

From the Saintes, we headed back north. We could sense that the voyage was near its end, but there was still excitement ahead.

The next day, we tied up to the dock in St. John's, the capital of Antigua and Barbuda, a three-island English-speaking nation (the other island is an unoccupied rock, Redondo) with only 85,000 citizens.

As at a number of other islands, we were met by a local band, generally colorfully dressed people playing mellow Calypso-type music and pan bands, otherwise known as steel drum bands.

From St. John's, a typical slightly shabby Caribbean town with many tourist restaurants, bars and stores, we visited a nearby fort, but also took a tour to fabled English Harbor, the most important British naval base in the 1700s.

Largely abandoned for two hundred years, the landlocked harbor was rediscovered by the famed Nicholson family in the '50s and restored into a major historical living museum. It became the sailing capital of the Caribbean and home of the famous Antigua Sailing Regatta and Antigua Classic Sailing race.

I was later to know the area well when I lived there on my boat Selkie.

From Antigua we headed back towards Phillipsburg where we started.

The big excitement that night was due to a peculiarity of the ship's construction.

In addition to having a steel hull, its four tall masts were also steel. This is unusual as you don't want to have much weight aloft in a sailboat as it makes it heel more and you want to keep as upright as possible.

One of those masts was hollow and served as the exhaust for the diesel engine. Over time, carbon and tars from the engine condensed in the relatively cool interior of the mast, and on our last night, they caught fire spectacularly.

Flames and sparks were shooting out the mast like a giant Roman candle while crew members tried to extinguish them by aiming a stream of water from the top of an adjacent mast, which was maybe 40-ft. away.

Did I mention that the windjammers didn't sail from U.S. ports as they didn't meet American safety standards?

It all seemed like a great show to all of us who has become well-lubricated on our last night at sea.

I suppose they got the fire under control, for we arrived in St. Martin safely the next morning.

Some of us who had made friends had a last lunch together in Phillipsburg, and the nice lady who had been so friendly tried to figure out how we could escape her jealous husband to no avail.

Even so, it was a great vacation.

A trip to Hedonism

Perhaps my most bizarre trip to the Caribbean was the week I spent at Hedonism in Jamaica.

I discovered that I would be on the east coast two weeks apart, and decided to visit the Caribbean. I asked my secretary to book me something interesting; I was too busy to deal with it. I thought she'd choose Club Med, then basically party central.

Much to my surprise, she picked Hedonism, a even more adult version of Club Med.

After a hectic week helping promote computers, I found myself on a plane flying from Miami toward Montego Bay on the north coast of Jamaica.

It was amazingly clear, and we could see much of Cuba as we flew over it, enjoying tropical drinks to get into the mood. Then we started our descent into Montego Bay on the north coast of the island.

Just before we were supposed to land, we flew into a dense low cloud and couldn't see anything. Neither could the pilot.

Those were the days before instrument landings, at least in Jamaica, and he pulled up abruptly, leaving my stomach behind.

He made a slow big circle, and we looked back and saw that the cloud had moved on, but when the tried to land, it had settled there once again.

Once more, the pilot passed, and as we rose, announced that if we didn't make it the next time, we'd have to return to Miami.

I wondered why we couldn't just land in Kingston, but fortunately, we were able to land through light clouds and found the airport bring and sunny.

Soon I collected my modest luggage – I had checked my business clothes in the New York hotel I'd return to – and climbed into the resort's VW bus for the trip to the west of the island.

As soon as I sat down and opened the window waiting for the driver to collect other passengers, a local stuck a large joint, there called a spliff, in asking if I'd like to buy some ganja.

Not a prude but not being a smoker of anything, I politely demurred. He wasn't offended, but just offered me a cold beer. That sounded good, and I traded a dollar for the first of many Red Stripes I would drink on that vacation and in the future.

It was a pleasant ride along the coast to Hedonism on the west coast. I though I recognized some scenes from one of my favorite flicks, *The Mighty Quinn*, which was filmed on Jamaica and has a killer soundtrack as well as wonderful overacting by all.

Hedonism seemed a typical beachfront all-inclusive resort, and I was escorted to my small cottage. I opened the shades and found I was looking out on a nude beach.

I later found that part of the beach was clothed.

Not surprisingly, Hedonism was popular mostly with couples, with an excess of misguided men and relatively few women, most of whom would not stand out if conservatively dressed.

The food was typical resort buffet fare, and not only was wine, beer and cocktails, but even cigarettes.

The resort had many planned activities, including an infamous "picnic" to a nearby small island, but not much mischief unless you brought your own or were a young stud or female.

I did meet some nice – at least friendly – people there but nothing remarkable.

Locals wandered up and down the beach offering crafts, souvenirs and drugs of various types. It was cheap, and the guys couldn't believe I wasn't interested. Just not my thing.

One guy bought and ate a whole "tea cake" and reportedly was out for two days, rather a waste of his vacation money and time, I'd think.

Near the end, we took a tour to a famed viewpoint where a "tea room" was selling magical mushroom tea and tea cakes, basically brownies loaded with marijuana, for $2 or $3 each.

I did buy a cake and nibbled a corner, which had a large and fast impact.

I gave the rest away.

At the end of the five days, I headed back to cold New York. I had had a pleasant, relaxing time but that's all.

Sailing aboard the Mandalay

My next Caribbean adventure was with a former girlfriend we can call Jan on a sister ship to the Polynesia, the slightly smaller and more elegant three-masted schooner 236-ft. former yacht Mandalay. It held only 80 passengers.

We joined a two-week cruise that had started a week before in Grenada.

Our departure point was Saint Lucia, and we flew into the capital Castries. Literally. In those days, the airstrip was also the main street leaving town. They dropped gates on the road to keep cars out when a plane – a small turboprop – landed.

They have a big international airport now, but it's far out of town. Not as much fun, either.

We had a reservation at a hotel near Gros Islet at the north. It has a large modern marina filled with charter yachts and hosts a famous street party or Jump Up.

We made reservations at a restaurant not far away, but as we walked along the dark road, I stepped into a massive pothole and badly scraped my leg. The joys of the Caribbean.

When we got to the restaurant, they helped me bandage if after dosing it with some rum. It hurt like hell, but my leg soon healed and the tropical rum drinks eased the pain...

The next day, we were supposed to meet the ship, but directions were a bit vague, and no one seemed to know where we'd catch her. We knew it was at Gros Islet, but she was too big to come into the harbor, and this was in the days before cell phones or the Internet.

We should have found someone with a marine radio and called the ship. Instead we went to a place some people thought likely, a restaurant with a cock in the canal leading into the harbor.

Eventually, we saw the ship drop anchor, a small boat headed in to the harbor and we were able to flag her down.

In retrospect, it was a mistake to join a party that had been bonding for a week, as we were outsiders who never were fully accepted to the other passengers.

The accommodations, food and routine on the Mandalay were much like the Polynesia, but since I had a companion, it was more fun.

One complication was that I had met another lady just before leaving and I thought she was the one I wanted to spend my life with. That tempered some of the pleasure of the tropical adventure, and it turns out I probably should have stuck with Jan :)

We arrived on board in time for an excursion to Fort Rodney on Pigeon Point, an important historical site. It was in the surrounding bay that Admiral Rodney kept his Caribbean fleet before sailing off the whip the French.

The next island north is a gem, perhaps the most sophisticated island in the Caribbean (excluding St. Barts.)

Fort de France, the capital of the French department (state) of Martinique boasts a historic and elegant downtown with snappy dressed people, beautiful Creole women and fancy shops. It also has restaurants of the highest quality serving the best of seafood preparations, produce and fine French wines.

After exploring Fort de France, we anchored in a small bay to the south, where we ate lunch in a local restaurant that had partly collapsed into the sea so that we were at an angle and the water occupied part of the room. The chef walked out into the water to retrieve our lobsters...

The best-known place on Martinique is the town of St. Pierre, once called the Paris of the Antilles, on the north west. It was destroyed in a cataclysmic volcanic eruption in 1902 with only one survivor, a poor soul locked in an oven-like stone jail cell.

St. Pierre is worth exploring; the volcano is behaving these days.

Leaving Martinique, the next island north is Dominica, an English-speaking republic not to be confused with the Dominican Republic.

Little known and visited, it's the "nature island," with no large hotels and relatively few visitors.

As the north is a river that you can cruise in a native canoe and enjoy a lunch or rum. We tried that, but also climbed high into the mountains having to traverse a stream bed when the path disappeared, until we got to a waterfall at the top.

This is a high, rainy island where you encounter the native flora and fauna. Mountain chicken (frog) is a specialty, but Perdue is more common.

Next was another visit to the Iles des Saintes, and another great trip ashore and a fine lunch at the home of a shopkeeper's mother.

She didn't speak English, we little French, but had a great seafood feast. When it was time to pay, however, she only took Francs and we had only dollars and traveler's checks. Don't even think about credit cards!

Eventually, she called her son, who came over and took our dollars at an unfavorable rate...

Then on to Antigua once more, and Montserrat, my last visit before it exploded, and Nevis and a visit to Nevis Plantation again before heading back to St. Martin.

It was a wonderful trip even if I wasn't as good a companion as I should have been.

Sadly, the Windjammer Barefoot Cruises went bankrupt in 2008 following a tragedy when one of its ship and 31 crew members were lost in a hurricane. No passengers were aboard.

The Mandalay is once again sailing with former Windjammer managers on a similar regimen in the Grenadines. The Polynesia is sailing in Portugal, its original home.

Sailing on the Star Clipper

The next time I sailed in the Caribbean, it was quite a step up from the modest Windjammers. I sailed with my new wife Susan, the one I had met just before sailing on the Mandalay.

And the ship was the relatively luxurious Star Flyer, a newly launched ship based on the fast ships of the past. Unlike the others, it was a barkentine, with square sails of its forward mast and fore-and-aft sails on all four masts.

Boy, could she sail. We almost never maneuvered under power, but did 12 knots, a very fast speed under sail with the only sound the bow slicing through the sea.

Everything about the boat was better, from the cabins to the food to the wine, but it still provided the same casual good fun and adventure.

We started in Phillipsburg without our luggage, which didn't catch up until we got to Antigua. The islands we visited were too small for airports to deliver them or timing was simply bad.

That wasn't a big problem, as we bought T shirts and shorts from the ship's store, and comfortable garb on the islands, and washed out our underwear at night. We were newlyweds, after all.

We visited St. Barts, Statia and relaxed on St. Kitts where Susan had her hair braided into cornrows by a native lady on the beach. Unfortunately, it was very uncomfortable, and she anxiously undid the effort that evening.

We found that the bartender at the beach bar there was from Chicago. He didn't even try for a local accent!

Again, they had arranged for local bands to join us as we sailed between islands, and with Susan along, we danced much more in the evenings as well as enjoying the sensations and views.

The crew even caught some fish and bought fish and tropical produce at some of the island we visited, so the food was much better than the "international" pizza and spaghetti and meatballs of the Windjammers.

On Nevis, I was sad to see a giant Four Seasons rising on the northwest shore. It provides jobs and a boost to the economy to the poor island but I'm afraid that huge development has changed the sleepy isle forever.

In every port, we ate lunch, and I tried to find local food. That was sometimes challenging, for the restaurants have learned that most tourists want familiar fare and imagined tropical food like coconut shrimp and teriyaki chicken with Daiquiris and Piña Coladas.

We ended up at Antigua again, and we took another – for me – tour to English Harbor. I fear she liked the beach more than history, however.

We had to return to San Juan on a puddle jumper into the small airport on the French side of St. Martin. We stayed overnight and had a romantic dinner at a beach restaurant before flying home.

Sailing alone on the Star Clipper

When I sailed on the Star Flyer with Susan, there were many single people aboard, and when Susan and I split up after a short marriage, I decided to sail it alone.

This time it was the almost identical Star Clipper but there were only four singles aboard this time, two other men and a woman none of us took a fancy to.

However, I made friends with some nice couples and joined them on trips ashore and meals most of the time.

This time, we had a French captain and a Jamaican cook, and we joked that it should have been the other way around.

In truth, the food was fine, including fresh fish the chef bought in town and even caught when we anchored – you can't catch a fish doing 12 knots!

The captain was charming, and a bit reckless. She sailed so close to Diamond Rock off Martinique that the yards overhead almost touched the stark rock.

That rock just off the southwest coast of Martinique has an intriguing history.

During one of those endless and frequent wars between the French and British, the English fortified the rock with sailors, guns and provisions, dubbing it HMS Diamond Rock.

The immobile ship was a major thorn to the French until they secretly dropped some rum barrels off, making them look like flotsam. After the Brits got into the rum, the French were able to conquer the small isle with little fanfare.

We once again visited many of the same ports – most people don't take repeated cruises, I suspect – but on St. Lucia did thoroughly enjoy the famed jump up, though we learned later that it wasn't recommended. Crime was high then – not any more – and some tourists were killed in a robbery gone wrong.

The island population doesn't like people killing tourists, and the culprits were sentenced to be hanged, but the British Judicial Committee of the Privy Council commuted the punishment; though independent, the former English islands still used that as the ultimate court. They have since set up a local court for Caribbean nations, though only some use it.

A highlight of this trip was a trip by van to visit Marigot Bay on St. Lucia. It's the a perfect tropical dream, a tiny bay with a few modest beach inns, restaurants and bars under the palm trees.

Dr. Doolittle was filmed there.

Back on the ship, we sailed by Marigot Bay, which you could barely make out, and by the impressive Pitons, two perfect cone-shaped rocks at the south of St. No anchoring in that tiny anchorage for sure!

Escape to Paradise?

A Year in Antigua with apologies to Peter Mayle, author of *A Year in Provence*.

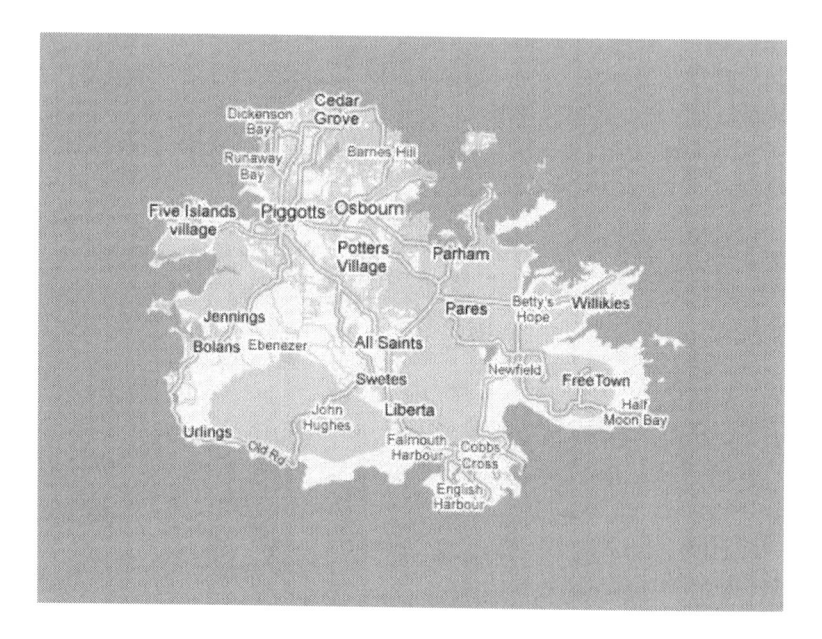

How many workaholics in Silicon Valley have dreamed of chucking it all and sailing off into the sunset?

Almost all, it appears. But few do. Mortgages, kids and fear deter most of them.

Not me. I did buy a boat in the Caribbean, but in retrospect, maybe I should have stayed home.

I encountered a litany of problems: a boat that wasn't ready, crew abandoning ship, crazy shipmates, a blown engine, a sinking and then the final indignity, a fate shared with Humpty Dumpty. Nevertheless, I don't regret the experience — even if I wouldn't go through it again.

In my case, fate told had me it was time to go.

I was burned out. Former client and 3Com president Bill Krause wasn't the only one to advise me to quit after 10 years, but he was right. Unfortunately, I didn't take the advice.

After 15 years running a successful public relations agency with mostly great clients like Hewlett-Packard and Silicon Graphics, I could hardly stand to go to work. I hated to talk to clients. It was agony to pick up the phone to call reporters and pitch stories, even to long-time friends in the media.

My second marriage had ended after only two years, but fortunately, my former wife was an excellent PR person who had worked with me. She started her own business, taking the clients she had served, allowing me to leave without excessive guilt.

I had to sell my house, and though I took a loss, it still provided a decent payout from earlier houses that had appreciated.

My retired Army colonel father died, an especially poignant event because we had finally started to become close after a lifetime almost as strangers. But he surprised me by leaving a legacy. Though not large, it was enough to let me pursue a lifelong dream.

All these factors convinced me to leave the 9-to 5-working world.

A new life

I left business, and started freelance writing. It was a natural because of my past life as a writer and editor. It also appeared the ideal business for someone who wants to live aboard a boat and make a bit of a living and gain a certain amount of respect and perks — though it's not as easy as nonwriters may imagine. There's far too much competition. It seems as if everyone wants to write, especially about travel, sailing and food, three of my great loves, so it's difficult to break into the business and get worthwhile assignments. Nevertheless, I knew I could exist for a while even without much income, so I decided to take the big step.

As it turns out, though I sold a few stories, that time was the only period since I was 18 when I didn't have enough income to pay taxes – even with interest and dividends from some investments.

I thought of two long-time desires, moving to Italy or Mexico for a bit, but I finally decided to pursue a life-long dream: To sail for an extended time in the Caribbean. I had sailed for 35 years, owned a number of boats, and thought I was realistic about my ambition.

Starting in May, I began to research possibilities.

I formerly had an eminently suitable 38-foot Pearson 385 cruising sailboat for ten years, but had sold it a few years before largely due to uxorial pressure.

It was just as well. It's a long way from California to the Caribbean, my cruising grounds of choice. I was more interested in being there than sailing there, a long and arduous voyage that would have included treacherous weather off Central America, a thousand-mile slug upwind in the Caribbean along dangerous coasts, and far more time and patience that I have.

In truth, my ideal cruise is 20 or 30 miles to the next harbor to enjoy the local life, food and location for a bit, then another short cruise.

Other options open to me included buying a boat in Florida, where the selection is excellent and the complications few, but it's still a long way from Florida to the heart of the Caribbean, almost 1,000 miles upwind.

Why not just start where I wanted to be, in the Leeward or Windward islands? There are plenty of boats there, many belonging to people who thought they wanted to sail around the world, but got stalled on a tropic island when the wife or girlfriend — or the skipper — said "Enough!"

A cursory search indicated that was true. There were many suitable boats available cheaply.

After talking to acquaintances at sailing publications (I had once been contributing electronics editor of *Sail*, *Motorboat* and *Marine Business*) and doing some research, I found that there were lots of brokers and boats in the Northeast corner of the islands, in the Virgin Islands and Sint Maarten/St. Martin, the peculiar island half Dutch and half French.

There also were plenty of boats in Martinique and Guadeloupe, the French being avid sailors and their government then encouraging sailboat production. Not speaking French, however, or enchanted with the style or construction of the popular French boats, I decided not to pursue a boat there.

Surprisingly, that left few markets for boats. I couldn't find any other serious brokerages all the way down to Trinidad. There were obviously boats for sail — the joke among sailors is that every boat is for sail — but no significant organized markets.

The obvious choice

The exception was Antigua, notably its English Harbor, a world center for sailing. It is home of famous Nicholson's Caribbean Yacht Sales and irrepressible Jol Byerley, famous as a raconteur who also wins almost every race he enters with his crew of lovely topless blondes.

A few faxes and phone calls later, I was convinced that there were suitable boats available, and at reasonable prices — plus plenty of others at astoundingly high prices as well.

That being the middle of the hurricane season, however, I decided that it would be prudent to wait to go looking.

It was fortunate that I did. Hurricanes Luis and Marilyn blew through the area in September. They devastated parts of Antigua, as well as all of St. Martin and St. Thomas, two of the prime locations for yachts. It's estimated that 600 boats were destroyed -- or at least substantially damaged -- in Sint Maarten's Simpson's Lagoon alone, for example.

Needless to say, the hurricanes affected the market, substantially reducing the number of boats available, but also putting a lot of damaged bargains on the market.

The hurricanes knocked out communications, never excellent in most of the Caribbean at best in those days before the Internet became ubiquitous. One of my prime broker prospects, Nicholson's Caribbean Yacht Sales, was without consistent phones or fax for two months.

When I finally reached them again a few weeks after the hurricane — by mail — they suggested I wait a bit to visit.

Finding crew

In the meantime, I embarked on a search for a crew member to accompany me since I had no interest in cruising alone.

I should diverge here to talk about crew. Most people who want to go sailing have a partner. Those who don't usually try to find one. Many people like to sail alone, but I don't, both to share duties and have company.

Just as important, having another person aboard is simply basic good sense. If anything happens, from falling overboard to being injured, that other person can literally make the difference between life and death.

Having said that, it's not critical to start with another experienced sailor, just someone who wants to learn and is fit and able. More important is attitude and compatibility. Even a 40-ft. boat can be very small if you're sharing it with someone who grates on your nerves – and it can happen very quickly in such a space, particularly during the inevitable times of stress: anchoring, going into slips and docks, in shallow waters among coral — or even when the wind is simply blowing hard or not at all.

So the other person was very important.

As a divorced man in my 50s, I had been looking for the right woman anyway with little success, so decided to concentrate on simply finding a compatible person. Ads in local sailing newspapers, on the Internet and in Bay Area personal columns turned up many leads, too many to completely follow up. Choosing the most likely, I met a number of prospects, none just right.

The most likely was a divorced woman in her late forties who was ready to leave her paralegal job and the area for an adventure. She also was a walking advertisement for cosmetic surgery and decoration, having tattooed eyeliner, mascara, lip coloring and a most impressive chest; she'd never drown. After a few dates, however, it was clear that our interests and priorities were too divergent. Fortunately, she made life easier for me by realizing that herself. She abruptly called and said she was moving "back east" where a girl friend had asked her to visit.

Her name was Susan, same as my second wife. Remember that. It's significant to this story.

About this time I discovered that a young female friend — not a girlfriend or potential one, but an experienced and adventuresome sailor — was ready for a break.

Annie was 26, an artist and photographer, upbeat and curious about the world. She had been a serious member of the Sea Scouts for 15 years, making a number of trips up and down California, a long and demanding passage. We had also sailed together briefly, and I knew that she not only knew her stuff, but really liked sailing and wanted to do more than her part.

She was also cute and flirtatious, but though I had originally met her at a Trader Joe's with other thoughts in mind, we had dealt with that and I basically regarded her like a daughter -- or at least a niece. She's a very mystical and spiritual person (unlike rational me) who is interested in almost everything except dining out or socializing, which I am, but we compromised.

Annie had just split up with her boyfriend, and had been doing temporary work by choice, so it was a good time for her to take some time off, too. After discussing it, she agreed to join me for three months.

With Annie signed up, I abandoned my search for crew. I figured I'd find someone in the Caribbean before she left after three months on my boat. Boy was I wrong!

But it was time to find a boat.

The search for a boat

By mid November, the islands had recovered from the hurricanes enough that it was time for me to visit and look at boats. I considered a long-term charter, but they simply didn't make sense. Boats like I wanted chartered for $1,000 to $2,000 per week, prohibitive for months, I thought at the time, though I learned better later. And I didn't think it made sense to try to find a boat on my own. There were too many islands, too many boats. I decided I had to use a broker.

I contacted yacht brokers in the British Virgin Islands and Antigua again since those on the other islands were hopeless at that time. I received lists of available boats, then requested detailed fact sheets by fax of the most interesting prospects.

Then I arranged to fly to Antigua first, which I thought a less-promising location, then on to the B.V.I., where a friend from long ago had invited me to join him and his wife for Thanksgiving dinner.

I had plenty of frequent flyer miles from many trips and much money spent on my American Airlines AAdvantage Visa card, but discovered that I had to "spend" 60,000 miles for the trip instead of the 30,000 usual. The cheap seats were taken.

American then had a virtual monopoly on flights to small Caribbean islands and they all go through San Juan (and for Californians, Miami or Dallas). It's a long trip, but not unpleasant. You either fly overnight or arrive late at night. I arrived late, but had made arrangements with a hotel at English Harbor to let me in.

The V.C. Bird International Airport in Antigua is one of few in the world named after a living politician, in this case the father of the country, known to his subjects as Papa Bird (His sons now run the almost-totalitarian government).

The airport was originally built during World War II by American forces, which used the then-British island as a base for hunting German submarines and protecting the Panama Canal. The airport has since been improved, but baggage still seems to have a lot of trouble getting from the plane the short distance to the terminal after you climb down the staircase from planes – sometimes in the rain.

Finally retrieving my baggage, and clearing the inevitably surly customs and immigration officials, I found a cab for the half-hour trip across the island.

Antigua may have the worst roads in the Caribbean, and that's not a trivial claim. They have huge potholes, and no lights or signs, while unlit and unmarked repairs wait around each bend. Even in my exhausted state, I couldn't relax, but soon arrived at Nelson's Dockyard at English Harbor. After waking the porter sleeping on a bench outside my hotel, I was admitted to my room and fell asleep in a romantic bed with canopy. It was wasted on me, I'm afraid.

I had been to English Harbor twice before on large cruising sailing ships, but the Dockyard is always a treat. An 18th century English Naval base, it was abandoned in the late 1800s until "rediscovered" in the 1950's by an English sailor, Commander Nicholson, who subsequently organized restoration and started a charter business that grew into an empire that includes many local businesses.

Now a National Park of Antigua and Barbuda, an independent country with 85,000 citizens, the Dockyard has been turned into a living museum that caters to yachts instead of naval ships.

The complex features many sailing businesses, plus a number of restaurants and bars, and two hotels. I had chosen the less expensive Admiral's Inn, former engineering offices that have been turned into atmospheric rooms at reasonable rates. An alternative is the exquisite Copper and Lumber Store Hotel, a former warehouse with elegant individually decorated rooms.

As I walked out my door the first morning, I was reminded again why I love the Caribbean: the romantic setting, the blue water a few feet away, the warm sun, the clear blue skies, the unique aroma of exotic flowers and plants. Anchored outside my room were dozens of sailboats. Perhaps one would soon become mine!

After a breakfast that included tropical fruit (not local, it turned out; the hurricane wiped out most of the crops), I walked over to the yacht brokerage to begin the search.

The perfect boat?

Nicholson's Caribbean Yacht Sales is located upstairs in a small office in the old paymaster's office in Nelson's Dockyard. The office overlooks huge yachts tied stern to the quay. There, I met Norma Prudhom, an ample and delightful English woman who had sailed over with her long-departed husband many years ago, then stayed on to first help out in the office, then sell yachts. The 60-ish Norma, it turns out, lives with a wild-haired Rasta ferrier named Shadow, one of the surprises I was to encounter in this unreal land.

It being a quiet Thanksgiving week, the aforementioned Jol Byerley and his girlfriend/partner Judy McConnachie were out sailing; they're among the few people in the marine business who seem to continue to enjoy their sailing after a lifetime of working around boats. It was some time before I met them. More on them later.

Jol's wife/ex-wife (?) Jenny, a lovely and charming English woman, ran the bookstore below the brokerage. I bought some local books from her. I later learned that she lives with the leading yacht salvage expert on the island, a man I was unfortunately to get to know professionally. I would have rather gotten to know her better.

Norma had arranged for me to see a number of boats, mostly based on my stated interest. We discussed them, and I set some priorities, then we got into Norma's beat-up, four-wheel drive mini-pickup, heading first to look at boats at Crabb's Marina on the other side of the island.

Crabb's is the "wrong" boatyard on Antigua, being isolated on the Northeastern corner of the island on a large bay protected from the pounding Atlantic seas by treacherous reefs and Long Island, site of the exclusive Jumby Bay Resort, once noted as the home of Norman Leach, the host of "Lifestyles of the Rich and Famous." Jumby Bay charged $1,000 per couple per night, a bit out of my range.

In all honesty, Crabb's didn't look promising. Boats were scattered around a large field, and at first, all looked as if they had been badly damaged in the hurricane. As I got closer, I saw that they were actually fine. Crabb's digs holes with a backhoe for the keels of sailboats, an excellent arrangement that kept the boats from toppling in the strong winds. Few boats at Crabb's were damaged by Luis, while many at fancier English Harbor and Jolly Harbor were.

We looked at a number of boats, from a $18,000 mess that actually would have been okay if it were cleaned up, to a vastly overpriced 60-ft. schooner whose owner had a created a myth in his mind that he could sell the boat and live like a king elsewhere.

Crabb's boatyard reminded me of the Humane Society. Some of the boats seem to wag their tails, imploring you to adopt them, whereas others seem to have given up, and wait for the executioner's needle.

Abandoned boats that represented someone's dream slowly rot in the tropical heat, while others are carefully tended by people who still dream to someday sail off to Tahiti.

I worried for Norma, who panted and sweated in the hot sun and exertion of climbing into the boats, but she was tougher than I though. She just likes to eat.

Soon, we left Crabb's and headed completely across the island to Jolly Harbor. It was a only 20-mile trip, but on Antigua, that's an epic journey, over bad roads, taking unmarked turns and dodging dead animals among the potholes.

Jolly Harbor could be in Palm Beach. It's a completely modern, sterile development with hundreds of unsold condos, a newly dredged marina and a small shopping center catering to the crowds that haven't yet arrived.

Like so many developments in the Caribbean, it represents a dream for the developer that turned into a nightmare. Fortunately, its owner has the resources to follow that dream, for otherwise it would have turned into one of the many abandoned or fading resorts in the Caribbean.

At Jolly Harbor, we looked at the boat I had originally thought my best prospect. Ridiculously cheap for a 45-ft. ketch, it had started life in the North Sea, and it looked like nothing could ever phase it. A heavy, deep-hulled steel boat, it would never get anywhere quickly, but it also would plow right through the treacherous coral reefs that sink dozens of fiberglass boats each year.

Unfortunately, it didn't fit my expectations. It was just too primitive: no refrigeration, a tiller for steering instead of a wheel, minimal accommodations, a small engine that shook the boat like a wet dog, no arrangements for a shower, and a layout more suitable for cold Holland than the heat of Antigua.

Its owner, a sly Dutchman named Hans, ran the Marina. He had picked it up for a song, and expected to turn it over quickly. I later discovered that no one ever made money at Hans' expense, so perhaps I made the right decision in passing. We enjoyed a Heineken together, but no sale.

Then back to English Harbor. Norma was patient. We looked at a number of boats, some severely damaged in the hurricane, some just cheap. Many were at Antigua Slipways, the leading boat yard between St. Martin and Trinidad (excluding the French-speaking islands).

I had led Norma to believe that I was looking for a very cheap boat, but she then showed me a nicer one — expect for the hole in the side.

During Luis, most of the boats at the Slipways fell over. They had been up on jacks, and when one fell, the others tumbled like dominoes. That's why so many owners chose Crabb's the next season, to place their boats in the inelegant but safe holes.

Though it was shocking to see so many boats with split sides and large holes, the one I was most interested in had a different sort of damage: during the hurricane, it, like many others, had been tightly anchored close to the tenacious but flexible mangrove trees in the most protected part of one of the best harbors in the World.

Unfortunately, a large ferrocement (yet, concrete) schooner had broken loose and smashed into many other boats.

Time Lag, in particular had a hole rubbed all the way through an inch of fiberglass-reinforced resin at its deck line. Fortunately, because of the location, the only real damage other than to the top of hull were scratches and a twisted toe rail.

The toe rail is the extruded aluminum rail that runs along the edge of the deck, holding the boat together and providing an attachment for some important fittings and lines.

There was also some water damage; rainwater (not sea water) got into the boat, but by the time I got there, it was dried out and not a problem.

It didn't seem like a big deal, and the boat was a bargain.

Priced at $20,000 less than before the hurricane, and $40,000 less than a similar but older boat, Time Lag seemed like the right choice.

She was a Sigma 41, little known in the States but a hot racer well known and respected in England and on the Continent. Built in Plymouth, England, she was fast, well built and well arranged for cruising as well as racing. The boat had been at least as far as New Zealand, and certainly across the Atlantic.

Not surprisingly, she seemed like the perfect choice, even at twice what I had intended to pay. After all, even after I paid for repairs, it would be well under market price. I felt I could cruise it for a while, then sell it at no loss, perhaps even a profit.

I made an offer and canceled my plans to go on to the Virgin Islands to look farther. I've always been one to stop shopping when I find what I wanted, not seek the ultimate. This attitude drives most women crazy.

With that behind me, I relaxed for a few days while some paperwork was completed, never a quick process in the islands, even if they ignored the American Thanksgiving holiday and didn't take those days off.

I later realized that I had conch curry for Thanksgiving dinner. It wasn't very good. I like to eat local food, but I soon learned the truth of the old saying, "No one ever went to the English-speaking Caribbean for the food."

While there, however, I arranged to have the boatyard fix the damage and I gave them a substantial deposit.

I also explored the island a bit more and met more people. Most were pleasant, some very much so. I hung out each evening at the charming Galley Bar, an open-air hangout on the Harbor run by Marina Murphy, a local woman who I got to know well if superficially. She had an exhaustive knowledge of local herbs and plants, and we concocted the idea of a book about the plants and their uses, with drawings by Annie to illustrate them. It seemed a sure winner.

Soon, it was time to leave. After only six days in this foreign land, I had made one of the most expensive personal purchases of my life other than houses. I returned to California, announcing to the boatyard that I would return a month later at Christmas. I was happy but someone intimidated by the month ahead.

Leaving Silicon Valley

My next task was to wrap up affairs at home to prepare for an absence of six months to a few years. I was living in an apartment with only a month left on the lease, and the landlady assured me that there was no problem as long as she didn't lose money.

Intending to simplify my life, I sold some possessions, lent or gave most of my furniture to my daughters, and put others in storage. Since I had moved from a 3,400-sq.ft. house into a small apartment, half the work had already been done.

I had little trouble parting with things. They seemed to represent a life I wanted to put behind me, and I was happy to be rid of possessions that recalled painful memories.

I also had to buy certain things to take along, and I was probably West Marine's best customer that month, buying items I knew would be expensive or difficult or impossible to find in Antigua.

You can carry almost anything into Antigua for a boat, but if it's shipped separately, there are major hassles with customers and expensive duties.

I also had some writing assignments to complete. Having the editors change direction after the projects were finished certainly complicated work, but I was learning that free-lance writers don't have much leverage.

Annie was getting her life in order to take off, too. Since she had committed to join me, however, she had met a new guy, and become engaged. I feared that she would back out. That didn't turn out to be a problem; I didn't know at the time that this was the 26-year-old's fifth engagement. She had arranged three months off from the art classes she taught and looked forward to the experience.

Soon before Christmas, my daughter Wendy arranged a going-away party for me; many loyal friends came, including some that traveled farther than I think I would have.

Annie also had a going-away party where I met her fiancée, a nice programmer soon to suffer major heartaches.

We were leaving on December 26th, and Christmas was far from my mind. I was barely able to find gifts for my daughters, sons-in-law and granddaughters.

My kind first wife Teddy invited me to join a large and diverse group for Christmas Day, but I left the last dregs of my life in my apartment for my poor daughter Wendy and son-in-law Steve to handle. It was a rotten thing to do, but I was exhausted from the frantic pace.

The trip to Antigua the next day was pretty uneventful, though choosing to leave the day after Christmas wasn't such a good idea in retrospect (not that I had much choice because of limited space available for free flyers on the planes to Antigua).

The trip to Antigua

I stayed at a hotel near San Francisco airport that last night since we had an early flight — and I had already given away my bed. It wasn't a restful night, with unsettling nightmares about lost passports, lost money and lost tickets, a throwback to previous experiences.

Annie's fiancée Martin arrived early with her to pick me up, then drove us to SFO. We had eight very heavy bags, and I wasn't sure we could take it all with us. Turns out that there was no problem, though I had to pay some overage. I should add that I provided the tickets and all the living expenses.

I accepted that since I was much better off financially than Annie, and I knew that she wouldn't have been able to accompany otherwise. And I needed a crew member.

We had to spend a night and day in Puerto Rico — free flyers at Christmas time are lucky to get on the plane! — and ended up in a rather sleazy place near the airport.

I had a typical delightful Puerto Rican dinner of beans and rice and chicken and fried plantains but Annie has very conventional and limited tastes, a surprise for such an adventuresome person. She also doesn't eat seafood or tropical fruit, two of the attractions of the Caribbean.

Then we took a walk along the beautiful moonlit beach, and went back to fall exhausted to our rooms. Even my bleak room with its loud air conditioner and smell of stale smoke couldn't keep me awake.

This was the last time we had separate rooms.

The next morning, we took a cab into Old San Juan, a delightful place in spite of the tourists like us.

We had a pleasant morning, though a Federal government shutdown had closed the picturesque old fort that was our prime destination.

That afternoon, we boarded the flight to Antigua, landing at 4 p.m. with our piles of baggage. I hired a porter, and we unexpectedly breezed through customers.

The officer simply asked, "Do you have any gifts for anyone?" ignoring the bags full of expensive computer equipment, marine electronics and other possessions.

We then headed for the boat. Imagine my surprise when I discovered that in spite of a warning fax sent a week before, virtually nothing had been done on the boat.

Ironically, the only thing accomplished — that morning — was to remove many of the cabinets inside the boat to allow the workmen to remove the toe rail. We couldn't move aboard with the boat torn apart, yet this effort accomplished nothing until the new toe rail was on hand, ready to install. It would be a long time before that happened.

There we were, with eight heavy bags of luggage and no where to put it or stay.

Fortunately, I had learned some patience since leaving business, and discovered that there was a room available at the Admiral's Inn, a surprise at normally busy Christmas time but a legacy of Luis scaring off the tourists.

We stored part of the bags at the boatyard, then checked in.
Then began the long wait.

English Harbor and Dickerson Bay (background) from Shirley Heights.

A month at the seaside

Living in a small hotel room wasn't a very appealing prospect, so we soon moved into a pleasant if basic efficiency apartment on a hill overlooking Falmouth Harbor, a much larger bay about half a mile away from English Harbor.

It would have been better to get a place with two bedrooms since I was sharing the place with an appealing young woman who was just a friend, but none seemed available. It was also a bit expensive, but I thought it was just for a few days. I soon learned otherwise.

Though it was the end of December, the weather was generally pleasant. Some days were cool, windy and rainy, but certainly mild compared even to California's rainy December.

The apartment overlooked many large boats in the harbor. Some seemed as big as the QE2.

Colorful flowers and other plants complemented the blue water. We watched the mongoose hunt for lunch on the lawn while tiny bananaquit hummingbirds, the yellow birds Harry Belafonte sang about, dipped into the jelly I put out for them to eat.

It is frustrating to be in suspension, but we took the time to see the area and relax. I rented a small Jeep-like car a few times to see the island. Annie was a very enthusiastic companion, and fun to have around.

We met a lot of people. Because of the male-to-female ratio there among the visitors and sailors (about 10 to 1), Annie was especially popular.

The local busses were also an interesting experience. The cabs and the buses were both VW minibuses and many weren't marked. I asked someone how to tell them apart, and the answer was simple, "The ones with a lot of black people in them are busses. The ones with a few white people are cabs."

For a trip into St. John's, the seedy capital and only city on the island, the taxi fare was $20, the bus $1. The buses were a great adventure, barreling along with the doors open, stopping in the middle of the street for the drivers to chat with friends, people getting aboard with laundry and chickens, though I never saw anyone with one of the ubiquitous goats.

Unlike the situation in many countries, however, the local people didn't generally respond if you tried to be friendly. People on many Caribbean islands are shy and reserved, but on Antigua, many are surly.

Slavery ended officially 150 years ago, but they all seem to act as though you as a white person were personally responsible for all their problems. And they have plenty of problems.

The legacy of slavery remains a terrible blot even today. On Antigua, the slaves revolted a number of times, inviting draconian reprisals. Eventually, the slaves and their descendents reaped a sad revenge, arson. There aren't any historic plantations left as there are on some other islands, though throughout the island, abandoned windmills that once crushed cane serve as silent monuments to that dark period.

Antigua's planters freed their slaves before the other English islands, but only because they figured they're be better off paying the workers one shilling a day and not providing room and board.

Unfortunately, the people remained terribly exploited, working in insufferable conditions on sugar cane plantations.

The island really reverted to a subsistence economy until the '40s, when U.S. forces built bases on the island during World War II.

In the '50's, a local leader, V.C. Bird, now locally called Papa Bird, led a union of workers to fight for better conditions on the sugar plantations. They won, but it was a hollow victory. Soon sugar beets grown in Europe made sugar cane uneconomical.

Eventually, Bird negotiated independence from England. That former colonial power was undoubtedly pleased to rid itself of a impoverished troublesome reminder of what was once a fabulously wealthy colony.

Antigua remains fabulously beautiful, however. Even junked cars and trash can't hide the beauty, for nature in the form of hurricanes and rampant tropical growth always reclaims its due.

I later learned that the period I lived there was a dark one. For a ferocious hurricane had reaped vast damage to the environment as well as man-made structures. When I returned years later, the island was in much better shape.

We enjoyed the island's beauty a great deal. One day, Annie and I climbed steep Monk's Hill to see an abandoned English fort visible from the beach, but the path disappeared not far from the top. We didn't relish the thought of climbing through thorn bushes, high grass and the webs of huge local spiders, which are supposedly harmless but look like small snow crabs and are as vicious as corned rats.

When we got down from our fruitless climb, a local man told us the right way to get there, but it would have been a long trip around to the back of the mountain.

It was good to get the exercise anyway. We walked everywhere, probably 3 to 4 miles a day just doing routine shopping, phoning, etc., without any of the hikes like that one or to the beach.

I was probably in the best shape of my life with all that walking, plus some swimming and rowing once in a while. It was nothing to walk a mile to shop or go to dinner, but we learned to avoid the heat in the middle of the day, and occasionally took taxis, buses, rented a car or bummed from friends.

Soon, on one of the trips back from St. John's, I ran into three delightful young Australian women who were traveling around the world. I invited them over to meet Annie, and we all became friends.

One upbeat and outgoing, one intellectual and reserved, one perpetually unhappy, they were a strange trio out to see the world.

I was spending time with four young women, but it was like having four daughters around.

The three Aussie girls and Annie atop Monk's Hill.

I again became a tour guide, and took our poor rented car up one of the horrible roads — really a trail, to the top of Monk's Hill we had tried to climb on foot.

There are few more magnificent sites, yet this prime attraction remains overgrown and forgotten, typical of many historic sites in the Caribbean.

Eventually, the Ozzies met young men, then found work on sailboats and explored the Caribbean. Then they disappeared as do so many friends in the Tropics, never to be seen again.

When you vacation in the Tropics, a week of relaxing and exciting activity is delightful, but keep at it and it can be very boring. There was little I could do on the boat except prod the boat yard, but that had little impact. Instead, the days were spent sightseeing, visiting the beach, occasionally sailing on others' boats, and eating and partying.

The local food and drink
Few cuisines sound better than Caribbean food with its exotic vegetables and fruits and fresh seafood, but unfortunately, food on most islands rarely fulfills that promise.

This is especially true on former English and Dutch islands with a bland culinary tradition that even local spices can't overcome. As a result, the local food often seems to be overcooked animal parts and unidentifiable vegetables in spicy grayish-brown sauce, often containing gummy dumplings. Everything else seems fried. And many dishes are drenched in hot sauce.

Nevertheless, it is possible to find excellent local food, particularly on the French islands, and increasingly on others as the hospitality industry realizes that many people do value food other than hamburgers, steaks and fried fish typically served to tourists.

One problem is that many islands don't actually grow much food or catch much fish. Farming may seem a leftover from slave days, but the crops grown then were primarily sugar cane. The islands are generally great places to grow vegetables and fruit, and some islands do produce excellent produce.

Oddly, fishing isn't part of the culture in many islands. As a result, much of the fish, meats and even vegetables are imported from the states and elsewhere, often frozen in the case of meats and seafood.

On Antigua, for example, you could buy produce from local ladies at a small farmers market in English Harbor, or a larger one in St. Johns.

But for fresh fish, the best approach was to radio one of the local fishermen, who could supply what you need in many cases.

Among the local seafood are dolphin fish (mahi mahi or dorade), wahoo and huge marlin. Conch (conk), the huge whelk shell that symbolizes the Caribbean, is popular, but becoming rare because of demand.

Local spiny lobsters are, of course, the most popular treat for tourists, but many come from elsewhere.

You definitely have to distinguish the food locals eat from that of tourists, though KFC is very popular among locals as well as visitors!

Because the islands have been poor, much of the local food has been based on rice and dried bean (called peas) plus local root and other starchy vegetables as well as greens.

Chicken is probably the most popular meat, and though "lamb" is served to tourists, I notice a lot of goats and not many sheep on the islands…

Perhaps the most famous dish to outsiders is jerk chicken or pork, which is rubbed with a spice mixture containing allspice (pimento locally) or cooked over pimento wood. It can be very spicy.

On Friday nights, and on holidays, local ladies would set up 55-gallon oil drums as griddles, grills or fryers and prepare treats in their front yards. It was very tasty and reasonable.

The most popular local treat was probably the roti, an Indian-inspired rolled up flatbread like a burrito, generally containing potato and pea or lamb curry.

Served with chutney and hot sauce, it's the perfect inexpensive but delicious meal.

Another local treat, though a lot of trouble to prepare, is the flying fish sandwich. Fillets of flying fish are deep fried and served on rolls with a tartar sauce.

Creole sauces of tomato, onion, sweet peppers, celery and garlic sautéed in oil are served on seafood, poultry and vegetables from New Orleans to Trinidad. Only the proportions — and the amount of hot pepper added — varies.

Oddly in the hot climate, stews and soups are popular with locals. They believe the hot foods are cooling, particularly with hot sauce. A popular example is bull foot soup; another is spicy callaloo soup, made with a leafy green also called callaloo (New Zealand spinach or yin choi).

Common starchy vegetables include roots prepared like potatoes: cassava (yucca), dasheen (taro), eddo, yams (hard white or yellow roots, not Louisiana sweet orange potatoes) and sweet potatoes.

Breadfruit, plantains (vegetable bananas) and pumpkin (a hard squash) are fruits, but are prepared the same ways as the roots: baked, fried, boiled, mashed, scalloped or in salads and soups.

Plantains look like bananas on steroids. There are many varieties, and it's worth ask to make sure what you're buying. The green (unripe) versions are cooked for their starchy filling quality, the sweeter ripe plantains fried.

Rice is very widely eaten, too.

Other popular vegetables include okra, christophene (chayote), dried beans (pigeon, black-eyed, red, pink or black), carrots, corn and cabbage.

Many foods are flavored with coconut milk (liquid extracted from shredded mature coconut meat), lime, ginger and the inevitable hot sauces and peppers.

The Caribbean is famous for its spices, notably cinnamon, allspice, mace, nutmeg and cloves. Some grow wild, but not much on dry Antigua.

The Caribbean is justifiably famous for its fruit, many completely unknown outside the islands.

Antigua raises unique, small sweet pineapples called black pineapples, for example, and the mangoes, papayas and bananas grow and are served everywhere.

And then there's the hot sauce. Each island in the Caribbean has its own commercial and home-made hot sauces. All I've tasted are nuclear; use them with caution.

The strongest are simply peppers (Scotch bonnet is the hottest) with vinegar and salt. Some temper the fire with papaya, tomatoes, bell peppers, onion or garlic, and a few, like Tabasco from Louisiana, are fermented and aged, giving a distinctive flavor.

On Antigua, Susie's is the local sauce. It's yellow with flicks of red and so hot the boatyard workers called the scary catalyst used to harden fiberglass resin "Susie's." Local yard workers would tell tourists who asked if it was hot, "No, Mon, put lots on!" with expected results.

English food, including steak and kidney pie made with Guinness and Cornish pasties, were also popular.

See the last chapter in the book for more on the food and many recipes.

The local entertainment

Most afternoons at 5 p.m., a group of us gathered at the Galley Bar for a beer or two.

Because it was right on English Harbor, the bar attracted both liveaboards and visitors from charter boats based in Guadeloupe 40 miles south. It was an undulating group, with people arriving, then departing again and again.

At 6 p.m., some of those people, plus a larger collection of expatriates who lived on shore, gathered at the nearby the Copper & Lumber Store Hotel for the Tot Club.

A famous tradition thereabouts, it was started by former British Navy sailors who gather to toast the Queen with 2 oz of heavy Pusser's Rum each night.

Aside from my belief that the United States had the right idea in 1776, I never could cotton to downing rum like that, especially when most of the members considered it only a prelude to an upcoming evening of drinking.

I stuck to Carib beer, a light refreshing drink from Trinidad that occasionally became scarce when the Antigua government decided to push the local mediocre Wadadli or locally brewed Red Stripe, more popular because of its reputation than its taste.

The other popular beer is Heineken, which I can't stand. It's flavored with what I later learned is Brettanomycces yeast, which is rightfully considered a defect in wine.

The sailors call Red Stripe "Port" and Guinness "Starboard" after the color of their labels, which match running lights on boats.

With little else to do, most people sat around and drank, though once a week a good crowd enjoyed serious Trivial Pursuit, always fighting for the American or English versions, depending on their nationality.

Being one of those people who absorbs useless knowledge like a sponge, I was good at the American version, but always lost if they pulled out the British version.

After drinking rum and beer all evening while we were playing Trivial Pursuit, the winning team won a bottle of rum or free drinks. Just what we all needed.

Many local people live hand-to-mouth on Antigua, and that's true for many cruisers and expats, too. Many saved their money for drinks and ate on board or at home.

For others, the selection of restaurants was rather meager: Most are either cheap and mediocre or expensive and mediocre.

There were a few exceptions, such as Abacadabra, a restaurant run by brothers from Naples, but most of the "better" restaurants are pretentious rather than good.

That corner of Antigua has a strangely divided collection of cultures. I was a member of the "poor" cruising sailors, the couples and singles who owned and lived aboard their own 35 to 45 ft. sailboats. Some came and went, but others had settled in Antigua for company, comfort, lack of funds to move on or boat problems like me.

The second group was the expatriates and white Antiguans. Some were quite well to do and lived on island part time, while others were born there or had been long-time residents. The established and wealthy group kept mostly to itself, though they met others at the Antigua Yacht Club and for special occasions.

The locals (Antigua short hand for blacks, the whites being called "residents") included some who owned land and businesses.

Some of locals were delightful, including, surprisingly, the immigration and dockyard officials, as well as many local tradesmen.

Some black Antiguans have done well, owning businesses, land and residential property. Most, however, just got by working in the tourist and yachting trade.

Antigua, like most countries, has very strict rules to restrict foreign workers, a major hassle for anyone who wasn't a citizen.

Many people work illegally, both whites with technical skills and blacks from other, even-poorer places, islands like Dominica and the former British colony of Guyana on the South American continent.

All of these illegal immigrants slipped around hiding from the immigration and labor departments, and while I was there, a number of locally visible people were deported and even jailed.

As is true here in America, of course, many of the illegal immigrants are the most motivated and industrious. Managers constantly complain about problems with the local employees and their attitude and skills.

The final group in the area is derisively locally called the "yachties," paid crew members from charter and private yachts.

"Smaller" boats (under about 75 feet) are mostly sailboats because it isn't practical for small power boats to cross the ocean to get to Antigua, but many of the larger sail and power boats are incredibly luxurious. They generally have capable professional captains, but many hire crew members for their youth and looks more than their experience.

Some crew members are there for a lark, of course, complicating life for dedicated professionals. Some captains freely admit that part of the job interview for attractive stewardesses is to sleep with them and partying is part of their job.

Many of these young crew members are well paid with little to spend the money on but drink and drugs.

Unfortunately, Antigua was flooded with crack cocaine, partly because some government officials look the other way for a price when the island is used for transshipments of drugs.

It's a local tradition; government officials also reportedly helped the U.S. bypass the international boycott to ship munitions to South Africa. They also facilitated shipping weapons to South American drug dealers.

Cruisers and crew members shouldn't be confused with "bareboaters" who charter a boat for a week or so.

A great adventure for those aboard, they are objects of great amusement to experienced sailors who gather to enjoy their cocktails as the weekly sailors bounce off each other and the shore as they attempt tricky maneuvers like anchoring and backing up in the crowded harbor.

The party at Shirley Heights
Each Sunday night – and to a smaller degree on other days – a big party was held on Shirley Heights high above English Harbor.

The party at Shirley Heights got going about 4 p.m., with mellow music from pan bands (as steel bands are called locally).

The tourists pour in from cruise ships and island resorts, enjoying the beer, the rum punches, the music and the incredible views.

Looking down, you see English Harbor and Falmouth Bay displayed, full of sailboats and yachts that look like toys.

Off to the west is the island of Montserrat 20 miles away, and to the south, alluring Guadeloupe 40 miles on the horizon. Some people eat, though it's early, enjoying hamburgers, flying fish sandwiches and various treats. Mostly they drink.

As the sun sets, everyone searches for the almost legendary "green flash" to the west. The sun sets over Montserrat, and as it darkens, the active volcano there spews like a Roman candle, nature's own fireworks show.

That's when the mellow bands are replaced by thumping reggae and soca, played by wild-looking musicians with deadlocks that scare the tourists, though they're perfectly harmless. It's just their act, and a good one it is.

The tourists thin out, and only the locals and brave outsiders remain, many of the latter armed with one too many rum punches. After all, this is an island where the rum is cheaper than orange juice, Coke or beer, so expect strong drinks!

Fortunately, the weather in Antigua is almost always gorgeous, 80 to 90 degrees year round, dropping to the 70s at night.

In the sun, it can be hot, but step into the shade, particularly when the trade wind is blowing 20 to 30 knots, and it's magnificent.

The water is beautiful, in shades from turquoise to deep blue, with a temperature around 85 degrees.

There are palm trees and flowers everywhere. It's a generally very dry island, partly because the English colonists cut down all the trees to grow sugar cane, which then didn't have enough water to grow well enough to compete with other islands.

But it's rainy in the summer and the mosquitoes abound. They really bothered Annie, but I guess I'm too tough for them when they could go after her tender skin.

Antigua claims to have 365 beaches, one for every day of the year, and many are straight off postcards.

The beaches around English Harbor weren't outstanding, however. Some are attractive, but they're in enclosed bays full of boats that often discharge sewage directly into the water, there being neither local restriction nor pump-out stations.

Other beaches are unsafe because of the pounding waves.

Though theoretically illegal, toplessness is common among white tourists, though never on local women. Some beaches are so isolated that you can do what you want, but the rare crime on these beaches discourages most people from using them.

Antigua was hard hit by Luis but most of hotels and restaurants were repaired quickly. Unfortunately for the people, however, visitors were scared off by inflammatory reports resulting in a bad year for the island.

Everything is expensive in the Caribbean, but simple pleasures, no need for heating or a car, and relaxed life style balance things if you don't want to spend a lot of money.

Oddly enough, Internet connection cost about the same as in California, and basic cellular service was comparable except for the $5/minute for calls to the States, and $1.10 incoming and local. It's also pretty spotty, though the supplier says it's about to upgrade, a common theme in the Caribbean where "Man come soon" is the local promise soon learned.

Selkie "on the hard" with fiberglass wizard Jack.

The boat

During this month, Time Lag, soon to be Selkie, has been out of the water propped up with fragile-looking jacks and pipes.

The yard finally filled the hole worn in the side during Hurricane Luis, filled scratches, and painted the topsides.

It also painted the bottom with paint so toxic it's not sold in the U.S.; the underwater creatures here are amazingly veracious. The workers do great work, by the way. They just take a long time to do it. Most of that time is simply spent not getting around to it.

The problem on the boat that remained was a damaged section of toe rail, the 43-foot long aluminum extrusion that among other things, holds the deck to the hull. It was chewed up by the ferro-cement schooner and the yard couldn't find a replacement.

And though the boat could be launched (if not sailed) without the toe rail, all the cabinets on that side of the hull were out, making it virtually inhabitable.

We also had had a visitor on the boat, either a rat or a mongoose, called a "rat" locally. He had been enjoying food left by the previous owner, and we put out poison and traps to get rid of him.

We never found him, but he disappeared, whether from the poison or accommodations on another boat.

Otherwise, the boat was in pretty good shape, needing only minor repairs.

Selkie at anchor, where she usually was, with Peter.

Selkie was a Sigma 41, a 41-foot-long English-made racer/cruiser with a good reputation for both racing and cruising. She's well equipped for both comfort and safety. She has bunks for seven, but that would be pretty crowded for more than a few days

While waiting for the repairs to be finished, we launched the inflatable dinghy (deflatable dinghy, some sailors call them for their constant need for repair), and putt-putted around the harbor. It was about a mile between the harbors in the open Caribbean, a rather scary ride in the small boat except early in the morning when the wind and seas were generally still.

Finally, a month after we arrived, the yard launched Selkie on January 25, just after my birthday.

As I prepared to move aboard from our little apartment, Annie announced that she wasn't continuing with me. She gave the excuse that we'd waited too long, but in truth, she met the dashing married Venezuelan chef from Merv Griffin's boat, took up with him, and eventually told her poor fiancée, who didn't hear from her for weeks. I did, however, since he had my e-mail and cellular numbers, but there was little I could tell him even if I had felt it my place.

Eventually, Annie announced her engagement to the chef, though that ended in less than two months.

A new crewmember?

With Annie out of the picture, I started looking for another crew member. There were many people available in Antigua, but I had many problems trying to find the right one. More on that later.

Anyway, I moved aboard the boat, and started fixing and cleaning. There was nothing major wrong, but it took weeks and there were still things to do.

While I was waiting, I figured I may as well refasten the deck, a cosmetic layer of teak plywood planking over the structural fiberglass. It turned out to be a horrible job, and in the process, I burned out a friend's belt sander. I had to buy another sander at a highly inflated price.

I learned skills I hope I will never use again, usually after doing things the wrong way six times.

Because I hadn't done this type of work before, I hired an illegal Dominican worker who claimed to be a deck expert. It turned out that he really was expert at cleaning and oiling existing decks and had no idea of how to do the work.

Through an error in communication, he thought he was getting $25 U.S. an hour, when the going rate was $25 of the local money, $10 U.S.

I actually paid him the higher rate the first few days, then when I discovered the error, he not only was sullen but worked at 40 percent of the rate he was before.

He also got mildly hostile, and I finally had to threaten to report him to the Immigration department to get rid of him.

Soon I replaced him with Marie, a sexy young French-Canadian woman I met one night waiting for a ride at the dock.

I first thought she might be a possible crew member who could even help me learn French. She was a careful and meticulous worker even though the work we were doing was very tedious — applying masking tape to both sides of 40-ft. long grooves less than 1/8th-inch apart, then filling the grooves with sticky silicone caulking.

Marie wanted to be paid daily, and I wondered where she was spending the money since any reasonably attractive young white woman doesn't buy many drinks or even meals on the island. Then I noticed her getting thinner and thinner, and sniffing a lot. Eventually, the local officials threw her off the island.

Every single electrical and mechanical item on the boat needed attention, even though the boat was in generally good shape.

The refrigerator, for example, needed new Freon and a filter, plus adjustment of the compressor belt (It operated from the engine, like a car air conditioner but has a cold storage plate so it's supposed to stay cold if you run the engine for 45 minutes twice a day).

But after that was done, the batteries didn't charge, so another technician had to come and replace the alternator belt and adjust it.

Fixing the pressure water required a new water relief valve -- a real challenge to find on Antigua -- and since it's a different type that the original, required three bronze adapters between the valve and heater.

The bilges, which had been full of disgusting black water (partly oil someone spilled changing the engine oil) required days of cleaning because of the inaccessibility and mess.

This is a continuing challenge on any boat, especially one being lived on in the tropics, and it turns out that there was a minor leak in the water pump that deposited about a gallon of sea water an hour into the bilge. Nothing dangerous, but annoying.

Unfortunately, fixing the pump later led to serious problems.

The engine ran but the oil, oil filters and fuel filters need changing. The fuel tank needed cleaning, another nasty job. In fact, almost every job on the boat was nasty.

The toe rail remained the biggest problem. The previous owner's agent asked the yard to order one in September, but it didn't do anything about it until December, or really seriously until after I arrived.

They finally reported that it was a custom part that was unobtainable. I later found that the rails were available. I should have hired a company in Antigua that specializes in finding parts rather than depending on a boat yard that didn't have a dedicated procurement operation.

Eventually, the yard found a similar rail, and after weeks of delay, a mysterious Frenchman who lives aboard an old tug containing a full machine shop installed the new rail.

It was a rough job. The supplier had cut the rail in half for easy shipping, and it had to be welded end for end, then bent into place. Not surprisingly, it kept popping apart. None of the mounting holes fit, either, of course.

The Frenchman kept muttering, "Zis is bad," which in English means expensive.

Ironically, the day the toe rail was finally in place, Rob, a nice South African guy working on his boat nearby said to me, "I don't know if I should mention this now, but I have a piece of that rail." He eventually gave me an unused 16-ft. length. I would have probably saved $2,000 if I had had it earlier, considering both the cost of the rail and the labor.

Other things that needed fixing included the anchor windlass, roller furling, safety life lines, instruments and dinghy. Plus much cleaning and minor work.

Desperately seeking sailor
All this work on the boat took a great deal of time and money, but I had bought the boat so cheaply I thought

it worthwhile. During this time, I was watching out for crew as I worked. In addition to word of mouth and Internet ads, I posted notices on convenient bulletin boards in the Dockyard.

The first likely prospect, a Canadian psychologist again named Susan, was close to my age, had completed an extensive English sailing program, and wanted to cruise.

Unfortunately, she decided that if we were going to sail, it would turn into a relationship and she couldn't handle a relationship, being a recent widow. I was pretty motivated to find a crew member, but realized it wouldn't work.

She, like Annie, was very mystical. She also had the annoying habit of challenging me as if I were a patient, perhaps trying to cure problems I inherited from my parents and 55 years of living.

I met a number of people who seemed likely prospects, but all wanted jobs, not free cruising positions.

I wasn't interested in just hiring someone to sail with me. It's odd — in California, people assume it would cost them money to go sailing. In Antigua, they assume someone should pay them to do it...

Then, one Sunday night, after many rum punches at the weekly party at Shirley Heights, I met a woman named — guess — Susan who seemed perfect.

She was a professional crew member but looking for a six-week pleasure cruise before a job. She was also not a kid (45) and seeming fun to be with. I invited her to move aboard, which she did.

In retrospect, the experience was a lesson never to drink more than one rum punch a day in the tropics.

Susan proceeded to take over. She rearranged things, bought exotic and expensive food and started to plan everything. The she decided she should tell me some things. Slowly. Over four nights.

First, her visa had run out, and instead of renewing it as they usually do, the authorities had asked her to leave the island. By tomorrow.

Not to belabor the point, the reason she was asked to leave was that the Antiguan government didn't want to treat her any more. She had been in the local funny farm, where she landed after freaking out in jail, where she ended after being arrested with her crack-dealing Rastafarian boyfriend José ("Arrested 27 times, but never convicted").

José had recently started a fight with a very big very drunk Irish crew member and after getting smeared across the floor, threatened to come back with his cutlass and chop him up.

It turns out that Susan was manic depressive, and thinks that lithium prescribed by her doctor interferes with her body, so won't take it. After seeing her violent reaction to a few minor incidents, I'm convinced she should take the medicine.

She also volunteered the information (unasked and with no immediate need to know) that she has herpes I and II, and thinks she should have an AIDS test since Jose gets around...

Anyway, I decided that I couldn't handle worrying about being chopped up or having my throat cut, so I said it wasn't going to work out. She threatened to hit me with a winch handle, but left, shipping out on a marginal training boat desperately in need of crew (Marie had been an earlier member of its party.)

I later saw her once or twice when she slipped past immigration onto the island, but fortunately, she didn't follow through on her threat or else she didn't have a winch handle handy. Of course, I made sure to keep my distance. And in all honesty, she seemed pretty calm. Maybe she had changed her mind about the legal drugs.

Next, I met Peter, a very Brrritish but sane guy my age.

Peter needed a place to stay a few days. Like the man who came to dinner, he stayed a month.

He was skilled and helped out in many ways. He also thought there was only one way to do everything — unfortunately not usually the way I wanted to do it. He would follow me around the boat recoiling lines after I had just coiled them.

At first, he did some work to pay his board, but after a while, decided I should pay him as well as providing a bunk so stopped contributing.

Peter came along on the first few sails around Antigua. Selkie sailed magnificently, handled well and was clearly fast.

As the time approached that I could start cruising, the lack of crew was clearly frustrating me.

Ironically, I met many nice and compatible people around English Harbor, and started to feel at home.

I missed female companionship, but English Harbor is not the place for a bald guy in his mid 50's to meet women — unless he's very wealthy and lets everyone know it.

It's a paradise for women, however. They may seem fat, ugly and old in Los Angeles, but they'll probably end up with a 25-year-old hunk in Antigua!

I finally realized that maybe my fate was to live aboard, not cruise around.

At about this time, my computer died. I had dropped it a few months earlier, and though the hinges broke, it worked for two months before I had to pay $866 to fix the computer.

At this point, I had been there about four months. I flew to California for a week to see family and friends, then returned to get ready for the famous Antigua Classic Regatta and Antigua Race Week, when at least one friend was visiting.

I left Selkie in Peter's capable hands while I was gone. When I returned from California, we moved Selkie to a pleasant anchorage off Admiral's Inn in English Harbor, a short row from shore and the Galley Bar.

It had been a quiet season in Antigua after hurricane Luis, but things were starting to pick up a bit as the season wound down and boats gathered for the weeks of racing and partying. It was a pretty relaxing life, but I was starting to get bored. Soon I was to wish for boredom again.

There had been a slow leak in the boat since I bought it, no problem except that we had to remember to run the pump once in a while to get the water out of the bilge.

I had mostly overlooked it, but Peter, being meticulous, spent a lot of time, and finally discovered that the water pump that sucked salt water into the boat to cool the engine was leaking. Boat engines have complex cooling systems, since salt water is very corrosive, so this sea water actually cooled a plate attached to the engine's radiator since the actual coolant was fresh water and solvent that circulated through the engine.

Now that I knew what the problem was, it started to annoy me, like a scab you can't help picking.

It didn't look like any big deal to replace the seal. In fact, the pump was almost the only part of the engine that was accessible without a major effort.

So I took it off, pulled out the seals, little rubber doughnuts that were in bad shape, and dinghied over to the local marine chandlery. Surprise: No seals of that particular type.

In fact, there weren't any on the island, and, even worse, the pump on the engine didn't belong on it. Someone had changed pumps sometime in the past, probably on some island where they couldn't get the right part.

Now I was in a fix. I couldn't run the engine to move the boat to shore, and without an engine, I couldn't charge the batteries or run the refrigerator. What looked like a simple job was turning into a major headache.

At that point, I went over to one of the few marine engine specialists on the island, Seagull Services, run by a somewhat inscrutable Dutchman with a huge red beard and orange jumpsuit.

Amazingly enough, he had the pump that was supposed to be on the engine, so I went back and replaced it.

I soon started the engine and everything worked fine again. Congratulating myself for work well done, I charged the batteries and refrigerator so I could have cold beer, then went about my day.

Unfortunately, the next morning when I started the engine to chill the refrigerator (supposedly only needed twice a day), the engine made a sickening clank and quit.

Why go through the painful memory? It turns out that the pump was on a faceplate that was easy to remove, but you were supposed to leave the plate in place and only remove the pump itself, a very difficult operation. Pump alignment was critical in this engine — a stupid design by any measure — and on top of that, I hadn't been given a special thick spacing gasket when I got the pump (I got it too late).

The pump had exploded, shooting pieces that stripped gears, bent the camshaft and done all sorts of other damage.

Any competent engineer would have designed a baffle to keep this from happening, but no one every praised English engineering. Nevertheless, it's hard to lay blame. It was an expensive lesson in diesel mechanics for me; what I learned: hire someone to do it for you.

We had to remove the engine to confirm the worst, and that mean removing all sorts of panels and the companionway ladder, opening up the bowels of the poor boat. It gave me a chance to thoroughly clean and paint the bilge, but I had to buy a reconditioned engine; repairing the old one would have been at least as expensive. It also had to be shipped in from Florida, a major hassle and expense.

It would have been a nightmare without the my friend Jac Housewright, a Southerner who runs an offshore investment business, sells yacht insurance and provides various help to sailors. I'll be eternally grateful for his help then and many other times.

The boat was a mess again, torn up as it had been for three months previously. I had her towed over to the boatyard so I could have electricity and easily work on her, and put her partway back together so I could live aboard. Peter found an assignment and moved off the boat, good since we both were getting on each other's nerves.

I was beginning to think I shouldn't have changed the boat's name, a move that supposedly brings bad luck.

It was obvious that I wasn't going to be doing much sailing anytime soon. I had long ago given up racing in Race Week.

I certainly wasn't a qualified racer, and though Selkie could easily be handled by two people under normal conditions, she took a trained crew of about nine to race.

Given time, I could probably have arranged a crew, for the boat is known to be a good racer, but it took a lot of preparation.

It also would have required a substantial additional insurance premium and entry fees, and likely some new sails.

I abandoned any thought of racing my boat, and was too preoccupied to sign on another boat. Instead, I spent a month and a half waiting for the engine, then getting it installed and working.

Fortunately, a lot of excitement keep me busy in the meantime. In a few weeks, the Antigua Classic Yacht Regatta arrived.

Most sailors know about Antigua Race Week, a delightful ordeal of nonstop partying and take-no-prisoners racing, but for me, Classic Regatta the week before was much more fun.

For the Classic, about 60 old boats and modern replicas race in a gentlemanly fashion befitting these floating antiques.

Some of the most famous names in sailing compete, if gently since they can't all stand the strains of modern racing with its high-tech materials and bloodthirsty sailors.

Since I was more concerned about Selkie, I forgot to arrange a position until very late, then ended up on the slowest boat in the fleet, but definitely one of those that had the most fun.

It was Lista Light, a pre-war Norwegian fishing boat as rough as Ticonderoga was elegant. Clamps held the rail together, and the mizzen boom had been patched with old boards and wire.

Lista Light's captain was an attractive, even provocative women in her early 50s. She had sailed from England in this relic assisted by a crew of inexperienced young people, mostly men in their late teens and early 20s. It was the reverse of every old guy's dream!

The first day of racing, the wind was so light that the poor heavy old girl could hardly move. We ended up finishing with only a few minutes to go to the deadline, and all the other racers, even the committee boat, had retired hours before.

The second day, we had more wind, but were still so slow that we ended up missing a mark and sailed straight through the serious boats, barely avoiding being sunk.

It was a great, if scary, photographic opportunity, but unfortunately, I stuck my finger through the shutter when I was changing film as the boat lurched, putting me out of the photo business for the rest of my time there.

The third day, I couldn't race since I had some work to do on my boat that couldn't wait. Apparently, it was a great day, with enough wind to intimidate many of the big guys to reduce sail while Lista Light found her element. Unfortunately, the crew had to pump her full time — old wooden boats tend to leak when they work hard.

Of course, sailing around a course isn't all there is to yacht racing. Gentlemen or not on the water, these guys know how to party. Many are old enough to know their limits, which means it can be a great deal of fun.

Rum companies sponsor many of the parties, and there are a lot of rums made in the Caribbean. The best are from the French islands, where they make it from sugar cane juice, not molasses, but the English won't admit that.

Antigua's local rum, Cavalier, is best mixed with fruit juice or Coke, and the English dismiss light Bacardi from Puerto Rico as Spanish rum.

They consider heavy Pusser's from Tortola or Mount Gay from Barbados the best stuff, and people will almost kill to get the distinctive red Mount Gay caps given out at the parties.

The companies also give away T-shirts, but of course, everyone wants to wear old hats and shirts from faraway races, not from the current year.

One of the highlights of the Classic Week was an elegant formal award dinner and dance; I actually put on my blazer for the first time for that one.

Sunday afternoon, tea on the lawn at the Admiral's Inn overlooked vigorous rowing and sailing competition in small boats, but the main objective seemed to be to swamp your competitors.

In all, I've rarely had a better time than that week.

Antigua Race Week
A few days later, Antigua Race Week began. After the previous elegant week of Classic Yacht racing, this was Animal House on the water.

These racers were serious, with rigs that stretched rules and finances, and hoards of young men bursting with testosterone and beer.

One boat was sunk because it wouldn't give way, a woman was killed because of a gear failure, and the races went on.

It was windy, great for the bigger boats, but terror for the small ones feeling the full force of the Caribbean.

The parties were rowdier, but if you weren't on a boat, you definitely felt left out.

The first day, I accompanied my friend Jac on his luxurious power boat as he followed the racers around the island to where they ended and partied.

Dickenson Bay's beach was a mile-long party, jammed with booths selling local food and drink, interspersed with reggae bands surrounded by speakers the size of small hotels.

It was a wild scene, but harmless. Everyone was having a good time, though I suspect those who had to rise early the next morning and head out into the Caribbean might not have enjoyed it then.

After two days of racing, the crowd took off on May 1 for Lay Day, a name fitting in more ways than one.

The partying started early in the morning with silly competitions suitable for fraternity parties, but I can't deny the day was fun.

From the beer drinking competitions to the wet T-shirt contests, which allowed male participants for the first time, we watched from Jac's trawler in probably the best location on the island.

The T-shirts came off, of course, but that was just a starter. Later were real fuzzy navels drunk from the source and a lot of young and not so young women providing entertainment for grateful young and not so young men.

That day, my visitor from the States arrived. Mike had planned to come to race, but between my problems and his business, arrived late.

He still had a chance to enjoy a few days in the tropics. He's a serious sailor, however, and was frustrated not to be able to sail.

He also missed his girlfriend at home; I'm happy to say they married not too long after he returned.

Mike and I did help some friends deliver a 72-foot ketch, Olivia, to St. Croix and St. John, a 140-mile trip. The last 10 miles, we hove to in a fierce squall since the harbor in Christiansted isn't one to enter when you can't see!

Mike was about to swim ashore through the fog since he had a flight the next morning, but fortunately, we checked with some boats in the harbor and found it wasn't fogbound.

We sailed in, tied up to a pier, then explored the town. The short visit to St. Croix reinforced my belief that the American Virgin Islands aren't representative of the rest of the Caribbean. You may as well visit Los Angeles or Miami and save your money rather than going there.

The next morning, we sailed over to St. John, still in the American Virgin Islands, only 40 miles away. It was a beautiful sail in perfect sailing conditions -- windy but not too windy, and perfectly clear.

We anchored off what turned out to be a nude beach, then went in and visited the small town. St. John is largely a national park, and the town has little charm.

The next morning, I took the ferry to visit a friend who lives on nearby Tortola in the British Virgin Islands about ten miles away. He maintains a consulting business in the islands, working part time in St. Thomas in the American Virgins, which has good communications.

He spends the rest of his time in a beautiful house on the mountain overlooking the West End of Tortola and much of the rest of the American and British Virgin Islands.

It's one of the most thrilling sights I've ever seen.

The British Virgins are well run and prosperous, with generally friendly people and natural charm except in Roadtown, the capital. They also have excellent stores and services, partly a result of the many charter companies that make their home there.

Returning to Antigua by air, I decided it was time to leave the islands for the season. After Race Week, Antigua's sailing season stops, and this year, the hangover from Luis made things even quieter than usual.

Considering the fast-approaching hurricane season and lack of crew, I decided to return to San Francisco for the Summer.

Come fall, I expected to return, hopefully to sail south.

Little could I have anticipated what Poseidon had in store for poor Selkie.

The ominous year
I spent the summer in California.

I didn't have a real place to stay, but stay much of the time on my daughter and son-in-law's "extra" house in Santa Cruz.

I also stayed in a few friends' places while they were gone, and in my time share in San Francisco.

I didn't do much, though I did write some.

One morning, I received a chilling call. A friend called to tell me my boat had sunk.

I had left Selkie securely tied in mangroves in English Harbor with numerous anchors holding its stern away from the bushes.

I had closed all the valves that let water in and out the boat except two – the water intake for cooling the engine, and the outtake.

I had to leave them open for I had hired someone to check the boat out and run the engine to keep the batteries charged (and not deteriorate) while I was gone.

Unfortunately, an inexpensive clamp had failed, allowing water into the boat, and since no one was there to notice, it filled it enough for poor Selkie to settle to the bottle in about 10 feet of water.

Ironically, the man who noticed and called me wasn't the one who was supposed to check on the boat; I suspect the man I hired wasn't checking as often as agreed, but it didn't matter.

Fortunately, the local salvage worker raised her quickly, not even waiting for my payment. They also attempted to save everything they could, removing and drying covers, sails, etc.

Selkie wasn't under water long – perhaps less than 24 hours, but that was long enough to destroy electrical equipment, electronics, cushions and more.

Also fortunately, my insurance company paid for much of the repair work, and much of the serious work was completed by the time I arrived in the fall.

Returning to Antigua in the fall, I still had plenty to do, but soon settled into the same patterns.

I also continued to look for crew. Getting to be fairly well accepted locally, I was able to get some writing assignments, though they paid little if any. It was still fun.

I came back home for holidays, but finally had Selkie usable and I did sail around the island a bit, and also crewed on other people's boats. Selkie sailed well and fast; I'm sure she longed to head south – or north – to visit new ports.

I did run ads for crew, and a guy from Monterey and two women from San Diego decided to join me for April Race Week, though I warned them that we weren't going to race.

They all were nice; the women, including a professional boat skipper, decided to stay on land, but we, and a few other friends, decided to follow the racers around the island, and from there, we would take Selkie to Crabb's for the summer – no more mangroves for me!

The sail was mostly uneventful, though we noticed the Antigua coast guard boat wrecked on a reef outside St. Johns on the way.

Once at Dickinson Bay, which is mostly open to the northwest Caribbean – the wind usually blows from the other direction – we anchored and went ashore to drink, party and eat.

As we were eating, I noticed Selkie drifting, however, and barely got back before she was about to hit another boat. Anchoring is harder than it looks!

After this, the women departed, and we set sail/motor around the north of the island to Crabb's.

There wasn't much wind, and what there was headed straight for us in sometimes narrow channels, and we motored most of the way.

Getting there, we stripped the boat down, leaving her in the yard's hands for the summer. We took a taxi for a modest nearby inn on the water, had dinner and prepared to fly back to California the next day.

At that point, I decided enough was enough. I put Selkie on the market, and the broker advertisers her for sale in likely spots.

Eventually, an Englishman bought her sight-unseen pending a survey, and put down a deposit.

During the survey, however, as Selkie was hanging in the air from two slings, something slipped. She fell to the ground, splitting open the side and break the mast among other damage.

It also turns out that they boatyard was in receivership (bankruptcy) but my insurance company did pay me for the damage, and eventually two guys from Guadeloupe bought her, patched her up (it's easy to repair fiberglass so it's as good as new) and sailed her off for a new life.

Clearly I shouldn't have changed the boat's name!

Looking back, it certainly would have been cheaper to charter a boat and a few months would have been plenty of time to sail from island to island.

I did live aboard a boat in the Caribbean, however, and had some experiences I'll never forget (if a few I regret).

I wasn't cured completely, for in a few years, I chartered a boat for a sale in St. Vincent and the Grenadines, but other than that, I haven't been aboard any boat but a ferry since I returned from Antigua, and every time my daughter encourages me to get a boat, I get over it quickly.

From my time on Antigua

While I was living on Selkie on Antigua, I took the opportunity to write a number of articles about boats, people and other aspects of island life. Here are some of them. They reflect conditions in 1997.

Adela
Surely one of the most talked-about entries in the 1997 Antigua Classic Yacht Regatta, the 169-ft schooner Adela is a perfect example of the Spirit of Tradition category. She combines respect for the past with today's construction techniques, sails and equipment.

Helmed by America's Cup winner Dennis Conner, Adela clocked the best elapsed time in her class winning the 'Sintra Trophy' for Spirit of Tradition. In 1996 she averaged 12.36 knots to set the record for the 42 mile Guadeloupe Race, a record its captain, Steve Carson earlier established in 1979.

Today's Adela is the descendant of the Adela first built in 1903, then turned into a house boat in the thirties after an illustrious quarter century of racing and cruising. There she remained for 50 years until the present owner bought her remains to restore in 1993.

Unfortunately, as work progressed, it was clear that the old girl was in far worse shape than anticipated.

Built in 3-in. planking on steel frames that had deteriorated, the construction was not salvageable. This led to the decision to build a new steel hull following original plans except for an updated underwater profile.

The builders incorporated much of Adela's original hardware and furnishings, even using the old teak planking for the deck and many interior features.

Just as the work was almost completed, however, disaster struck. In October 1994, a fire broke out in the boatyard where Adela was being finished, destroying everything on deck as well as part of the stern and interior. The builders had to take the whole interior out and start all over again. Fortunately, they were able to save some parts, which were lovingly incorporated in the reconstruction. Their work completed, the new Adela was launched in May 1995.

Adela is 140 feet on deck with a 99ft. waterline and 25ft. 6 in. beam. Her main mast rises 160 feet above the deck, and her 16ft. draft displaces 227 tons.

Perhaps the most noticeable feature of Adela under sail is her unique foresail which is fully battened and has an immense roach. Captain Carson explains, however, that this design allows the relatively small crew to make passages using only the foresail and headsails, a huge advantage over a traditional schooner sail plan.

Adela was designed and built to cruise around the world, entering other races welcoming such traditional designs as they occur. Carson and his crew will be heading for the Pacific in 1998 but we look forward to enjoying the marvelous sight of her under sail in the Caribbean again prior to her departure.

America Twice Reborn

Participants and viewers of the Tenth Anniversary Antigua Classic Yacht Regatta were treated to a rare sight— not just one but two replicas of the famous yacht America, racing as gloriously as the original.

It's a sight few will forget.

Surely the most famous yacht in history, the America that inspired the America's Cup Races was crushed by snow ashore in 1942, but the two new yachts maintain her tradition.

Both yachts are wooden gaff schooners, and both look magnificent as they sail. There are significant differences between the two, however, and neither is an exact copy of George Steers' original design, but are adapted to present conditions and circumstances.

One, called simply America, was built in 1967 by Goudy & Stephen of East Boothbay, Maine for the movie *Sail to Glory*. She was financed by Schaefer Brewing Company, and built quickly but well with a basic interior.

Donated to Kings Point Merchant Marine Academy, she was sold to Friendly Ice Cream Company, then to an Argentine owner who spent $300,000 — her original cost — to convert her to a yacht. She was then sold to a Spanish aristocrat who found her upkeep a daunting task, and in 1996, Paul Deeth of Antigua bought her and spent a year restoring her to her present superb shape.

America, which ironically is registered in the U.K., measures 130 feet overall, 91 feet on the waterline, and displaces 99 gross tons. Her beam is 23 feet, draft is 12 feet and sail area an impressive 5,587 square feet.

She also has the original full keel, a feature designers found optimum for the split schooner sail plan. She participated in the Tall Ship Challenge across the Atlantic after Antigua Classic Yacht Regatta.

The other America — America USA — is a new boat, launched in 1995 at Scarano Boat Building in Albany, N.Y.

She is the dream of restaurateur Ray Giovannoni of an ambassador to inspire interest in sailing and act as an ambassador to yachting events in the U.S. and overseas.

Slightly larger than the other classic reproduction, she measures 139 feet overall, is also 91 feet on the waterline, but has a beam of 25 feet and draft of only 10 feet.

More authentic on deck, her most controversial feature is a modern fin keel, which reportedly makes her a handful in strong winds even without her 6,400 sq. ft. of sail.

America USA can be seen at boat shows and taking out novices for day sails, but she spent much of 1997 after the Classic Yacht Regatta showing the American Ensign cruising the Mediterranean and participating in regattas.

Because of the different configurations and ages, the yachts didn't directly compete in Classic Races, but both were outstanding additions to the racing pageantry, and a delight to everyone who saw them sail.

Zeeland — A Family Sails a Classic

Many couples dream of cruising with their families, but few ever do — especially when their children are young. Rob and Anne Heijmerink of the Netherlands, however, have found a way to live their dream.
With four children under 11, they're in the midst of a two-year voyage that's taken them south from Holland toward the West Indies on a great circle back home.
They left in July 1996, working their way through Madeira, the Canaries and the Cape Verde Islands before arriving at Barbados after a 16-day crossing.

They arrived in Antigua for the Classic Yacht Regatta after a leisurely sail through the Windward Islands.

The Heijmerinks picked a good boat for their voyages, but it required a lot of work to get her into shape.

In October 1993, they bought the Zeeland, a heavy 51-ft. ketch typical of traditional North Sea double enders.

The style is called a spitsgat in Dutch, though the Zeeland isn't a typical shallow-draft Dutch design tailored for the canals of the Netherlands.

Looking much like a Colin Archer ketch, she has a deep keel suitable for ocean-going. She's built for safety and comfort, not speed, and requires a force six wind and all sails flying to reach 8 knots.

Designed by De Vries Lentsch, the Zeeland she was constructed by the Bultjer Boatyard in Friesland in North Germany in 1959. She was reportedly the first yacht built by the boatyard, which is famous for its wooden fishing boats.

Initially, she was completely traditional, a heavy, strong boat that had no electrics, no winches, and only a massive tiller instead of the wheel that now steers her.

Before setting out on his Trans-Atlantic voyage, Rob Heijmerink did a lot of work on the boat, modifying her so he and Anne could handle the heavy craft without help. Now she can be easily handled by only two people. They also modified the interior, making it cozy but roomy, a result of its wide beam.

The Heijmerink's children aren't missing out on their lessons during the long voyage. Their 10-year-old son and 2-, 6- and 9-year-old daughters study in the morning, and of course, the voyage itself is a better school than any building on land could possibly provide.

They've all learned English from other children and hanging around other cruisers, too. During the afternoon, they read, play games, make things and draw. They also fish, often proving dinner for their family.

After Antigua, the family headed for Dutch Sint Maarten, then south to the other Dutch islands, notably Curaçao, where they put their children in school for a few months before heading for Haiti and Cuba, then up the Intercoastal Waterway to Halifax and across the Atlantic home. What started out as a one-year sojourn has turned into two, an unforgettable experience for the whole family.

Of course, the Classic Yacht Regatta was one of the highlights of the voyage for the whole family. As might be expected, the crew raced the Zeeland for fun, not to win. She came in a respectable third in the Classic Class A category and everyone aboard had a great time. The Zeeland proved that even a slow boat is fun in this unique race. The Heijmerinks won't be back for the race next year, but they'll carry their memories of it for a long time.

A Classic Gentleman and Naval Historian

If one person symbolizes English Harbour to yachtsmen, it's the late Desmond Nicholson.

Member of the clan that rediscovered the abandoned 18th century English naval base, who helped bring Nelson's Dockyard to life and to its present status as a world-wide magnet for sailors.

Initially a race to Guadeloupe and back to Antigua, The Lord Nelson's Regatta began as a chance for charter boats crews to have some fun at season's end when their guests had departed.

In 1967, however, Nicholson suggested racing in the waters off Antigua, and the race has since developed into one of the world's premier sailing events, Antigua Sailing Week. In 1987, the Classic Yacht Regatta spun off from this popular and highly competitive event and established their own regatta held one week earlier.

Nicholson has been around classic yachts his whole life. He and his family arrived in Antigua on the 70-ft. schooner Mollihawk in 1949, when he was 23. His father, Commander V.E.B. Nicholson bought the old boat for £2500 during the war for her linens and other furnishings, but after the war, decided there wasn't much future for his sons in England, so he set off for the Caribbean.

Squatting in the ruins of the old dockyard, they were soon asked to take out some guests of the exclusive Mill Reef Club, and that led to a lively charter business with their first guest in 1950.

He and his brother Rodney each had their own commands, and in 1954, he brought the 86 ft. schooner Freelance over from the Mediterranean with an all-female crew.

In 1957, Desmond met his future wife when a charterer brought along his daughter, and he soon was married and decided to stay home and mind the store. The charter business grew while Rodney and Desmond started Carib Marine and the Admiral's Inn.

In 1967, as he was swimming with some charterers in Freeman's Bay, he found some pottery and half an ancient stone axe. That sparked an interest in archaeology. Soon he had so many artifacts around the house that he helped form the Museum of Antigua and Barbuda, which is his full-time passion today.

Initially, he focused on the Museum in St. Johns, but is now concentrating on research, spending more and more time in the Dockyard Museum where he has helped completely reorganize the exhibits. His tall figure was a common sight there, often huddled over his computer.

He early taught himself programming so he could compile a number of historic and archaeological databases for researchers to use. These include the history of Antigua and Barbuda, marine and yachting history and even tombstone inscriptions.

A prolific and engaging lecturer on local history, archaeology and other topics, Nicholson was a speaker not to be missed. He also wrote many articles and booklets, some offered for sale inexpensively in the Dockyard Museum Gift Shop.

Jol Byerley, himself a local legend, summed up the Nicholson's impact succinctly: "Without the Nicholsons, the allure of the Caribbean wouldn't exist. They brought true classics — Mollihawk, Freelance, Maria Catherina — here and Desmond has never forgotten the pleasure of these old boats."

Report from Antigua Classic Yacht Regatta

It's one of the few yacht races where being overtaken is a thrill, for the boat passing you could be Ticonderoga, the famous 72 ft. Herreshoff ketch built in 1936, or Fleurtje, a 175-ft. three-masted schooner from 1961.

It's the Antigua Classic Yacht Regatta, one of the most exciting events in sailing. Held annually at English Harbor a week before the huge Antigua Sailing Week with its cutthroat racing and non-stop partying, the Classic Regatta is definitely a gentlemanly affair, as befits an event featuring floating treasures.

The 44 boats entered this year (1996) in the Ninth Regatta ranged in size from the 25-ft. cutter Polaris Jack to Fleurtje. The oldest boat was Dione, built in 1912, the newest modern classics only a year old.

Some of the entrants gleamed after extensive restoration and weeks of preparation, while others were rough workboats like Lista Light, a 50-ft. Norwegian fishing boat built in 1936 and once used to ferry escapees fleeing Nazism across the stormy North Sea.

The first day of the Regatta saw such light winds that Lista Light finished only 7 minutes before the 6-hour time limit on a shortened course.

The second day featured fluky winds, from calms to squalls that created great excitement on the boats, some unsuited for the stresses imposed by modern yacht racing.

The third and last day saw winds to 24 knots that allowed even the heavy workboats to fly, and showed that old boats can sail fast and still look beautiful.

Overall winner on elapsed time was Liberty, a 52-ft. gaff schooner built in 1924, but second-place Lil Iolaire, an engineless 28-footer built in 1964 and captained by Richard Street, irrepressible Irish son of cruising author Don Street, was clearly the crowd's favorite.

Besides the true classics, a number of "Spirit of Tradition" entries livened the action. These included the 135-ft. ketch Alejandra built in 1993 and Adela, a 139-ft. schooner built in 1995 with a fully battened foresail that looked like it escaped from a huge catamaran.

Adela, which was skippered by America's Cup winner Dennis Conner, provided the incoming fleet entertainment when it went aground in the well-charted mouth of English Harbor.

Of course, as in any Caribbean event, the parties abounded. Aside from sponsor English Harbor Rum, there were parties from Mount Gay and Bacardi rums to quench thirsts, plus an elegant Edwardian Dinner and party at local hot spot Abacadabra.

One night, there were sea chanties — some rather bawdy, many accompanied by sweezebox and banjo — at the local yacht club, which organized the Regatta.

A special treat was a Sunday afternoon on the green at the historic Admiral's Inn with High Tea and gig races at which half the fun seemed to be falling in.

Sponsors Wayfarer Marine, North Sails and Antigua Distillery deserve special thanks for helping the Ninth Annual Regatta succeed so well.

What is a classic?
Entries must have a long keel, be of moderate to heavy displacement, built of wood or steel and be of traditional rig and appearance.

Old craft restored with modern materials or new craft built to old designs, such as Whitehawk, patterned after Ticonderoga, are also eligible.

Antigua Sailing Week

Take-no-prisoners racing and nonstop partying in magnificent sites with great weather: That's what makes Antigua Sailing Week one of the world's premier sailing events. More than just a race, it's a happening, one not missed by knowing sailors.

Now the largest warm-water sailboat race in the world, Antigua Race Week began modestly in 1967 when 14 local charter boats got together to relax at the end of the winter season after the last customers departed.

In 1996, more than 200 boats competed in Race Week. Competitors included huge 70-foot maxi-yachts, hot one design boats like Melges and J boats, live-aboard cruisers and a growing fleet of chartered bareboats that allow wider numbers of sailors to participate.

Official Race Week activities began Sunday with a race from English Harbor in southeast Antigua to Dickenson Bay on the northwest coast. Spectators on land enjoyed a great view from Shirley Heights above the Harbor, prelude to a day-long party.

English Harbor is a perfect, land-locked refuge for boats, but Dickenson Bay boasts the palm-lined beaches travel brochures trumpet. It was the ideal site for a mile-long party in the evening that featured four reggae bands and shacks selling local food and drink, interspersed with many of the island's premier hotels and restaurants.

Each night during the week, in fact, there was a party for participants and spectators. Many of the parties were sponsored by rum companies that poured samples to promote their products, helping the crowd relax and mingle. They also gave out the treasured T-shirts and caps that celebrate the Week.

On Monday, the boats raced Olympic-style courses off Dickenson Bay. Tuesday, they beat into the wind and seas back to English Harbor, providing the adrenaline-pumping excitement intense racers seek.

May Day, lay day for races, featured rowdy competition between crews, from the tug-of-war to beer-drinking races, to the wet T-shirt competition, this year opened to male contestants to little acclaim.

The partying continued late, alleviated by Antiguan snacks from rustic stands set up by local people.

Thursday and Friday featured more exhausting races, with the evening parties somewhat subdued -- even young crew members eventually run down.

The week ended with prizes awarded on a hill overlooking the Harbor, followed by -- what else? more partying and dancing.

Another Antigua Race Week ended, letting all who participated recuperate but ready to do it all again next year.

All agreed: It wasn't just one of the world's best race series. It was one of the world's great experiences.

Sailing in the Grenadines

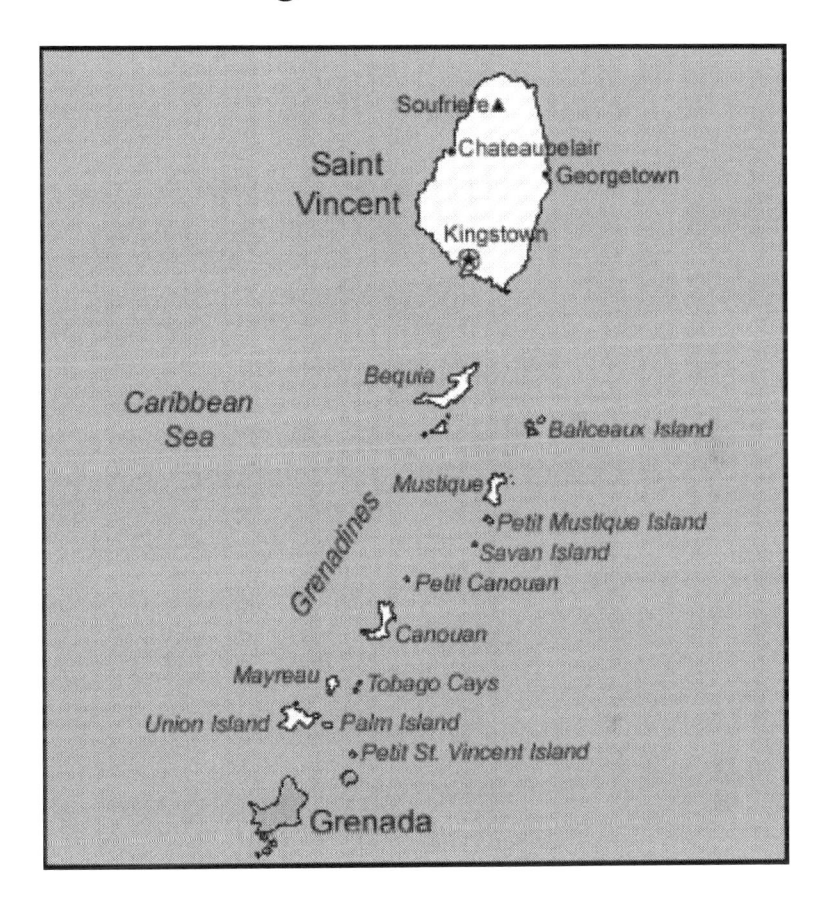

You'd think my adventure on Antigua would have cured me of the Caribbean, but a few years after I returned, that wanderlust hit again.

This time, I asked my old friend and sailing buddy Dave if he'd like to go sailing, cashed in some airline miles and chartered a 30-ft. boat in St. Vincent to tour the Grenadines. It was almost off season and I got a great deal.

If the British Virgins are the best place to start chartering, the Grenadines are second. A little more remote and less developed, with islands a little farther apart, they're beautiful and diverse.

The northern islands were given to the island of St. Vincent when the islands became independent from the United Kingdom, with the southern joining Grenada.

Dave and I arrived late, as always when you travel four time zones east, and took a cab to our modest accommodations over the charter company's facility. It wasn't a fancy operation by any means, but the boats was reasonably priced.

The site was in the far southwestern corner of the island, the site closest to Bequia, the first island in the Grenadines only 8 miles away.

We faced a channel looking at posh Young Island, a well-known luxury resort, and nearby on the mainland were a string of typical seafood and other tourist-oriented restaurants.

They were a bit of an anomaly since the island is principally an agricultural island and contains no large resorts, hotels or casinos.

We borrowed a dinghy and putt-putted to one of the restaurants for dinner. At the time, there was a lot of petty crime on the island, and the sailing club discouraged us from going far.

The food we had was typically Caribbean, fish and local vegetables and fruit plus been and some ill-advised rum drinks.

The next morning, we headed off from our adventure after stocking up on some provisions.

Bequia (BECK wee) is more of a sailing center than St. Vincent, but doesn't have an airport though frequent ferries delivery passengers and the occasional car to the small island.

The trip was most uneventful as we checked out the handling of the boat, drank a few beers and nibbled on some snacks as we got our sea legs. Well, bottoms.

The weather was perfect, the sun bright, the breeze fresh.

We had to round the far end of the island, so traveled considerably farther than 8 miles, but soon headed into the picturesque harbor of Port Elizabeth.

We could have anchored, but having had some bad experience with poor anchoring in the past, I liked the security of a mooring, so I rented one just off the beach. It turned out to be a great location.

We soon pumped up the dinghy and went ashore. There was no surf in the protected harbor, but we could also use a pier nearby.

Of course we headed for the nearest bar, which had a patio shaded by palm trees, and had a beer.

We soon got into a conversation with the proprietor, who had been the country's deputy prime minister and told us many interesting stories, including his inside knowledge that Columbus had really been a Portuguese Jew from Madeira, not an Italian from Genoa.

We then explored the small town, which didn't take too long, but it included some surprisingly complete markets and marine chandlers, a result of the thriving charter business nearby.

We decided to explore, then head out the next day, for there were many islands awaiting us.

However, the people were friendly, and we found the island very relaxing. We decided to stay another day.

We hired a taxi to give us a tour, and ended up at a modest restaurant on top of the island with views all over.

We walked the length of the town and harbor, and drank beer and a few rum drinks. People were friendly but it's not the type of place you can expect to meet single women – sailors are mostly men or couples and Dave was married anyway – but we ended up staying yet another day to check out a restaurant that was recommended and a bar with a good band.

Then both of us came down with a little stomach problem that discouraged us from sailing, but eventually, we did sail out around the other arm of the bay, stopping for lunch on the south side of the island probably walking distance from where we had anchored, then headed for fabled Mustique, the island of the rich and famous.

We were anything but, in our obviously chartered small boat. But after carefully avoiding an inconvenient shoal between the islands, pulled into the tiny bay at Mustique near Basil's, the world-famous (to sailors) restaurant and bar on piers over the water.

In fact, that was about all there was in sight. There was a tiny market and gift shop, but no cars and no other commercial establishments. We found out later that there was a swank guest house hiding among the palms.

However, ready for excitement, we cleaned up (the boat did have a fresh water shower), put on clean shorts and shirts and went ashore and to Basil's. It was about 4 in the afternoon and fairly quiet, but we were warmly welcomed.

I'm a bit reserved, but Dave is 100-percent Irish, and was soon talking to everyone, including a clearly wealthy women who has a house there. I should point out that only rich people have homes there, and some only use them a few weeks a year.

After eating and drinking together, she invited us back to her place. We hoped in her fancy golf cart and traveled up the hill, arriving at a palace complete with giant white columns surrounding the pool overlooking the sea.

There we also met her husband, which wasn't what we expected after all those rum drinks we three had consumed.

He was very nice, a fabulously wealthy Austrian or Swiss businessman, but after a while we decided to head home. It wasn't that far, and was all downhill, so we refused the offer of a ride and set out in the dark with small lights along what was really an overgrown path more than a road.

Halfway down the hill, we head music and laughter, and followed a path to what was obviously a fun places.

We wandered into what turned out to be the place the servants and workers of the islands gathered, and though we were the only white faces in the place, and couldn't dance worth a hoot, they were friendly and even bought us a few drinks, which we didn't need.

Eventually, we got back to the boat, where we remembered the name of the island – Mustique. The insects weren't a problem high on the hill with the breezes, but the harbor was awash with the little buggers, and we had no way to close the boat without expiring form heat and no nets. The insect repellant did help some.

The next morning, we went ashore, checked out and found a little more to see and had breakfast, then prepared to continue the voyage.

However, after talking a bit, we both agreed that we didn't have much ambition. If we sailed farther south to other islands, then we'd just have to come back and Bequia sure was nice.

So we went back, picked up the same mooring and relaxed for a few more days before sailing back to St. Vincent.

Once back, we did visit Young Island, then explored Kingston, the capital. There were few white people around, and we were hassled by an aggressive panhandler until an old man lit into him in the local patois we couldn't understand and he slinked away.

I wanted to visit the botanical gardens I had seen before, and thought it was a short walk, but it was a long way uphill in the heat, and we had trouble even finding some water to drink.

There, we saw a tree descended from one Captain Blight brought there from Tahiti, collected nutmegs that had fallen on the ground, and saw many interest plants as well as some birds and animals.

We also visited the inevitable 18th century fort, an impressive sight even after seeing so many others on the islands.

The next day, we headed back to California on the long flight. It was a pleasant relaxing vacation, but surely not the one I had anticipated when I booked a cruise in the Grenadines.

A return to Paradise

Before I moved to Napa Valley 17 years ago, I followed a lifelong dream. I bought a sailboat in the Caribbean and lived on it for a couple of years.

My plan was to sail the Caribbean from the start in Antigua, but my plans went seriously awry. Between crew problems, a blown engine, the boat sinking and other problems — you know you shouldn't change the name of boats, and I did – I never left the island in my boat.

Nevertheless I had a grand adventure, which you have read about.

Not surprisingly, I lost my taste for owning sailboats, and haven't been on anything aquatic but a ferry since except for a week-long charter in the Grenadines, an adventure in itself.

I thought about returning to Antigua, but feared the old worry: "You can't go home again." I figured all my friends would be gone, and the place completely changed.

Last fall, however, an old friend from Antigua visited Napa, and after visiting with her, I resolved to return. I did in January, coincidentally planning to be there for my birthday.

I was amazed to find that I had little trouble finding good free flights via the American Airlines AAdvantage program, though not at the lowest number of miles. Before I knew it, I was on the way.

The flight was delightfully uneventful, and I was able to make it with just one plane change in Miami.

Antigua is surprisingly far away, four time zones to the east, and I arrived grateful that Liz picked me up for the 20-mile drive (on the wrong side of the road) over roads even worse than Napa's.

She had a classic Caribbean bungalow on a hill overlooking Falmouth Harbor, a large protected bay that's become the home of yachting in the Caribbean.

I had my own suite with a bath – but warnings not to waste water on the dry island, for the public supply often failed and she had to then depend on a cistern.

The four-poster bed also had an ominous mosquito net around it.

I had rented a car for the next day, and planned to spend a few days as her guest, then travel on, maybe to charter a boat for a few days, maybe to fly down to Grenada or some other island I hadn't visited (there aren't many).

As it turns out, she had arranged a number of dinners with other ex-pat friends, and I realized that about half my scheduled time in the Caribbean was committed. So I had a Carib beer, walked to the nearby beach, and relaxed.

Liz is English, as are most of her friends – the now-independent island was once an English colony – and ran a successful business arranging high-end yacht charters.

She didn't deal with little boats like the 41-footer I had owned, but crewed yachts – mostly power – starting at 70 feet. Many were owned by very wealthy people who chartered them at outrageous rates for tax purposes or because they used them relatively little.

She spent much of the day on Skype and her computer talking to prospective clients, yacht crews and other brokers, so I went off alone to explore my old haunts.

When I lived there, historic English Harbor, a small, land-locked harbor, was the center of the yachting life, but the locus had shifted to Falmouth, a 5-minute walk away over a narrow neck.

Nelson's Dockyard at English Harbor, one a jumping area, has become a quiet museum, though a few restaurants, hotels, bars and shops remain.

Otherwise, almost nothing had changed. There was one small new inn, but other than a few proprietors changing and a few new businesses, it was just as I had left it.

To compensate for staying at Liz's – particularly for longer than I anticipated – I insisted on taking her out to lunches and dinners as much as possible.

Fortunately, she was able to break out at lunch many days and we enjoyed many of the local hangouts. Like many ex-pats, she doesn't really eat local food that much, but there is plenty of lamb and roast beef available.

The food was good, much better than I remembered. I ate as much local food as I could at the relatively fancy tourist-orineted places we frequented.

I ate everything with fins or shells I could find. We had local lobsters, grouper, mahi mahi, wahoo, shrimp and more, and when I snuck off for lunches alone when she was busy, had conch, flying fish sandwiches and searingly hot rotis, the Caribbean's version of a burrito.

The dinners she had arranged were great fun, and at them, I discovered many people I had known a bit. It turns out the local business community is quite stable; only the boat people move on.

I ran into a woman who sold me my boat now running a great bookstore, and had meals with the man who installed my engine after it blew up, the man who raised my boat when it sunk, the woman who made the cushions to replace those ruined by the sinking, and many others.

They were all delightful and gracious, welcoming me to a world that I couldn't enter when I lived on my little 41-foot boat.

I was even able to help Liz by writing some material for her web page and promotional material (Go to www.antiguayachtcharters.com and dream).

Too soon, I had to head back to Napa, itself a dream to most people. My return to the paradise I'd left was a trip that few could duplicate, but it's still a great place to visit.

Postscript: Sadly, just after I returned, a local San Francisco woman was killed at the very beach I frequented. No one knows what happened, but she apparently wandered away from a beach party into the rough terrain behind the beach. The police found the culprit, a transient from another island, quickly, but the news was unwelcome and certainly not typical of the fairly crime-free area.

Notes: People who live there call it the car i BEE an, not ca RIB e an. And they pronounce the island an TI ga.

Sailing in Antigua and Barbuda

The independent country of Antigua and Barbuda has 365 beaches, one for every day of the year, and each more striking than the next.

It also has more, and more varied harbors than any other island in the Lesser Antilles, some bustling with vibrant shore activities, some remote and unspoiled by man.

Some of the most enchanting of these isolated coves and bays lie among tricky reefs, but experienced captains can thread their way into spots no self-crewed charter and most visiting yachts would never attempt.

Though parts of Antigua attract budget tourists, most of the island is more attuned to upscale pleasures, and it offers much for visitors on yachts.

Though the food on chartered boats is often better than that served ashore, we've noted restaurants that might be of interest for variety, or to check out the bars at cocktail time.

English Harbor and Falmouth Bay

The yachting center of the island is Falmouth Harbor in the English Harbor area on the south coast of the island.

This protected bay is just a short walk across a narrow land bridge from historic Nelson's Dockyard in English Harbor itself, one of the most famous yachting centers on earth.

Hundreds of megayachts, both sail and power, visit or make their home here during the season. It has much to offer the visitor.

Nelson's Dockyard is perhaps the single most compelling historic destination among the islands from the Virgin Islands to Trinidad.

An authentic and lovingly restored 18th century naval base, it reeks of the age of sail when the French, Dutch, Spanish and English fought for control of the rich sugar islands.

In addition to being a museum itself, it boasts a museum that tells its colorful history. Many of the other buildings are just as interesting, even if put to modern use as hotels, restaurants, shops and yachting services.

Just across the protected harbor is Antigua Slipways, one of the major boatyards in the long chain of islands, and worth visiting by any lover of boats.

Far above the harbor is Shirley Heights, which offer breathtaking views to Montserrat 20 miles away, where eruptions of a volcano for the last 15 years have rendered half of the island uninhabitable, but often provide impressive displays for the earth's raw power.

You can also see the French island of Guadeloupe to the south and visit historic structures and an interpretation center that tells the area's background.

It's also famous for its weekly parties each Sunday, with smaller versions on Thursday and Friday.

Mellow pan bands (steel drums) play traditional Caribbean music until 7, when intoxicating reggae pulses start – with dangerous rum punches to accompany it.

Though Nelson's Dockyard attracts many yachts, most of the activity is in Falmouth Harbor, a major center of yachting with three large marinas, extensive marine businesses, and restaurants, clubs and shops sure to interest any visitor.

The food ranges from roti stands to sophisticated cuisine, with most offering local seafood and other treats. The bars and clubs are filled, some with crew from yachts, others with owners and guests.

Some boats anchor out in the large bay, providing convenience close by but a more peaceful environment.

From the area, you can also visit the island's capital city, St. John's, a bustling but not particularly enchanting city, especially when the cruise ships dock, or to other attractions around the island.

Southwestern coast
Also on the southwestern coast are anchorages at Carlisle Bay and Curtain Bluff, each featuring tony resorts with excellent restaurants.

Jolly Harbor
The west coast of Antigua is sheltered in usual wind conditions, making for relaxed sailing. The major yachting center here is relatively new Jolly Harbor, an extensive development with luxury condominiums as well as complete boat services plus restaurants, services and shops

Five Islands Harbor and Deep Bay
Harbor is a misnomer for Five Islands, for the large but protected bay is almost completely pristine. Anchor here, and you may feel like you're the only people on earth.

Just north of Five Islands is Deep Bay, a charming anchorage in front of a long sandy beach. It also is home to the large Royal Antigua Hotel, which offers many services and amenities.

St. John's
The bustling capital city of Antigua, St. John's, lies at the head of a deep but busy bay.

St. John's features many attractions for visitors in the restored and developed Heritage and Redcliffe Quays, which can be delightful when not overrun by tourists from large cruise ships that often call.

St. John's contains many restaurants and shops and is also the place to find many items not easily available elsewhere. The Museum of Antigua is worth visiting to help understand the island and its people. A modern shopping center lies just north of town.

Guarding St. John's is historic Fort James with impressive views, interesting exploration and a restaurant serving local specialties.

Dickenson Bay
After leaving St. John's, the harbors and bays of Antigua to the north and east are more of what one expects from a tropical paradise.

Long Dickenson Bay is the sort of place many tourists envision – endless sandy beaches filled with hotels, bars, restaurants and shops with partying each night.

The north coast
Rounding Antigua's northwestern corner, you enter the wild side of the island, which slopes generally south east. This is the windward side of Antigua, open to the force of winds that have blown all the way across the Atlantic. It is somewhat protected by an offshore reef and many islands, but is definitely off the usual tourist track and calls for an experienced crew.

The most famous site in the area is famed Jumby Bay resort on Long Island. A delightful anchorage, it also allows access to the resort. Nearby are other quiet anchorages, notably one on unoccupied Maiden Island, the perfect site for beachcombing.

Crabbs Marina lies on a peninsula on the mainland, as does the village of Parham with a sheltered anchorage, but few attractions for most visitors.

Large and wild North Sound opens beyond Crabb's Peninsula. Protected by reefs and islands and islets, if is the perfect place for quiet and privacy as well as observing the birds, exploring tiny isles and relaxing. It's hard to imagine anything more pleasant than enjoying fresh-caught fish grilled under the stars in such a lovely anchorage.

A narrow and winding passage leads out of the sound through the reefs, but for most yachts, this is a cul de sac. It's best to approach the rest of the windward coast from the south.

Southeastern Antigua

Just east of English Harbor is protected Indian Creek with its virtually landlocked anchorage. It's overlooked by the home of guitarist Eric Clapton, a local icon.

Mamora Bay contains the fancy St. James Club with full luxury facilities including numerous casual and elegant dining options, a spa and hair salon, plus horseback riding.

Large Willoughby Bay is almost completely protected by reefs, but offers little attractions for visitors anyway. It's just something to pass on the way to some of Antigua's best sailing destinations.

Uninhabited Green Island is Antigua's most eastern point. Though the island is private property leased to the Mill Reef Yacht Club, it has two delightful anchorages, and visitors can go ashore in certain areas (and all beaches in Antigua are public).

North of Green Island, the sound is protected by barrier reefs and you can anchor in what would appear unprotected waters.

NonSuch Bay is a large, protected bay perfect for exploring by dinghy or sailing in small boats. There is little development here, but Harmony Hall offers a bar and restaurant, art galley and gift shop in an old sugar mill, plus a fleet of fast Dragon sailboats for informal races.

A tricky channel leads north toward Barbuda, but most boats leave Antigua from other points.

Barbuda

Barbuda, a large island almost as big as its sister in Antigua and Bermuda, is one of the most unspoiled islands in the Antilles.

Once privately owned and used to raise slaves, livestock and produce, it was too dry for sugar cane, so was mostly left alone.

The island boasts few lodgings and amenities, but unlimited beaches, interesting bird life and geological features.

Though only 25 miles north of Antigua, its reefs and limited accommodations restrict visiting yachts, and bareboat charters are generally prohibited. It's ideal for those who really want to get away.

A Guide to Cruising in the Grenadines

The islands between St. Vincent and Grenada offer some of the best cruising experiences in the planet, from completely deserted anchorages in tiny uninhabited islands to colorful native villages to sophisticated resorts.

The Grenadines are split between the two former British colonies, with most attached to agricultural St. Vincent though three are part of Grenada.

They're all small islands, some tiny, and virtually everyone is dependent on visitors from yachts.

None of the Grenadines experience mass tourism, however. They're too mostly small and hard to reach to attract the Club Med or Love Boat crowds.

Grenada has a large airport (built by Cuba, helping spark the U.S. invasion!) with international flights, and St. Vincent has inter-island flights including to Puerto Rico.

You can fly in small planes to some of the islands, however, an advantage if you want to avoid a sail from Grenada or even St. Vincent.

Bequia is less than 10 miles from St. Vincent, while the most southerly Grenadine, Carriacou, is 15 miles from Grenada.

The people of Grenadines are famous sailors and were once whalers, and for many years they lived off the sea and their small fames. Now, most have prospered from charter and other yachting, and there are few other commercial activities.

St. Vincent has few attractions for visitors except an impressive botanical garden full of exotic tropical plants including a breadfruit tree perhaps planted from the fruit brought to the island by infamous Captain Bligh after he returned from his mutiny.

If visitors start in St. Vincent, it's only for the airport. Many begin in Bequia a short sail south.

Bequia
Though only 7 square miles in area, Bequia is the largest of the northern (St. Vincent) Grenadines. It's also one of the most charming.

It's what people envision when they think of a tropical island paradise. The main harbor, Admiralty Bay, is large and U-shaped, sheltered from the prevailing winds.

The bay is ringed with beaches shaded by palm trees, with modest bars, restaurants and shops hidden behind along a path.

In the evening, sounds of the Caribbean flow across the bay to boats anchored in turquoise water. The island also boasts many craftspeople and artisans, and their wares are offered in many places.

The main appeal for most visitors, however, is perfect uncrowded beaches where you can tie under palms, snorkel or swim. Most of the beaches have modest beach shacks where you can buy beverages and snacks or even meals.

Tours of the island can be arranged, and visit an abandoned sugar plantation now a restaurant, a refuge for sea turles, and magnificent views of surrounding islands.

Bequia does have a small airport as well as ferry service to St. Vincent 8 miles away.

Many visitors are tempted to stay a while, but if they want to move on, Friendship Bay, a sheltered cove on the other side of the island on the way to Mustique provides secure anchorage for a short stop or overnight.

Canouan

Unspoiled and virtually undiscovered, Canouan is one of the Caribbean's most up and coming luxury destinations.

It is less than 20 miles south of Mustique, and the three square-mile island is surrounded by small bays and coves, secluded white sand beaches and one of the Caribbean's largest coral reefs for incredible diving and snorkeling.

A short distance lie the Tobago Cays. Canouan contains a number of upscale resorts including Raffles.

Carriacou

Carriacou is part of the nation of Grenada about 20 miles north of that island. It is the largest island of the Grenadines. It has an area of 13 sq miles and a population of about 5,000. The main town of Hillsborough is the bustling heart of Carriacou, with banks, government offices and the main police station.

The island has a strong tradition of boat building, which continues to this day. Pre-Lenten Carnival, August Regatta, the Maroon Festival and the Yuletide Parang Festival have also contributed to its fertile heritage. More active than some of the other islands, it still offers fine beaches and pristine reefs for exploring, snorkeling, swimming and diving.

Renowned Sandy Island just east of Carriacou is a symbol of the ideal island -- pure white sand embraced by turquoise blue waters.

Mayreau

Mayreau is the smallest inhabited island in the Grenadines with just 250 residents; the island is around one and half miles long and midway between its larger neighbors of Canouan and Union islands. It has no airstrip, so all visitors arrive by boat

The island village has a few bars, restaurants and a small stone church. From the little Catholic Church, visitors have fantastic views over the neighboring islands including the picturesque Tobago Cays islands. Mayreau has several long sandy beaches, the best of which is Saltwhistle.

Musique
Mustigue is only a short sail from Bequia, but it's a world apart. The island contains relatively few vacation homes, many owned by celebrities, and only a few small inns.

Basil's Bar, a restaurant plus built over the water, is the only such establishment on the island, and local residents gather for cocktails nightly. The island also has some boutiques, many featuring colorful local arts and crafts.

Palm Island
Palm Island is a tiny island a mile from Union Island with an area of 135 acres but has five beaches. The island contains an exclusive resort and about 20 private holiday residences.

Petite Martinique
Petite Martinique is the southernmost island of the Grenadines belonging to the state of St. Vincent and the Grenadines. It is 2½ miles away from Carriacou. Its area is 586 acres and population is 900. The island is really one large hill with fine beaches on the calmer western leeward side. The residents of this island live by boat building, fishing and seafaring.

Petit St. Vincent

Petit St. Vincent, known locally as PSV, is consists of softly rolling hills spread over 113 acres surrounded mostly by two miles of white sand beaches. The island is privately owned and contains an exclusive resort with 22 cottages and a small restaurant.

PSV has been tamed just for the 22 simple yet luxurious cottages. Lying well off the tourist mainstream, PSV could be best described by what is not there. It has no airport, no formal check in, no keys. There are no televisions nor are there telephones in the cottages.

Tobago Cays
The Tobago Cays are considered one of the most beautiful places in the world by many well-traveled sailors.

The archipelago consists of five small uninhabited islands - Petit Rameau, Petit Bateau, Baradol, Petit Tobac and Jamesby – that form the Tobago Cays Marine Park, a national park and wildlife preserve run by the St. Vincent and the Grenadines government.

The park consists of a 1,400-acre sand-bottom lagoon that includes 3-mile long Horseshoe Reef.

Union Island
Union Island is the southernmost island of the Grenadines belonging to the state of St. Vincent and the Grenadines The island is home to approximately 3,000 residents. The island has a small airport with flights to St. Vincent and some of the Grenadines and international flights to Barbados, Carriacou, Grenada and Martinique.

Due to its volcanic silhouette, it is also called the *Tahiti of the West Indies*. The island is approximately 3 miles long and 1 mile wide. The highest peak is Mount Tabor, which rises 1000 feet above sea level.

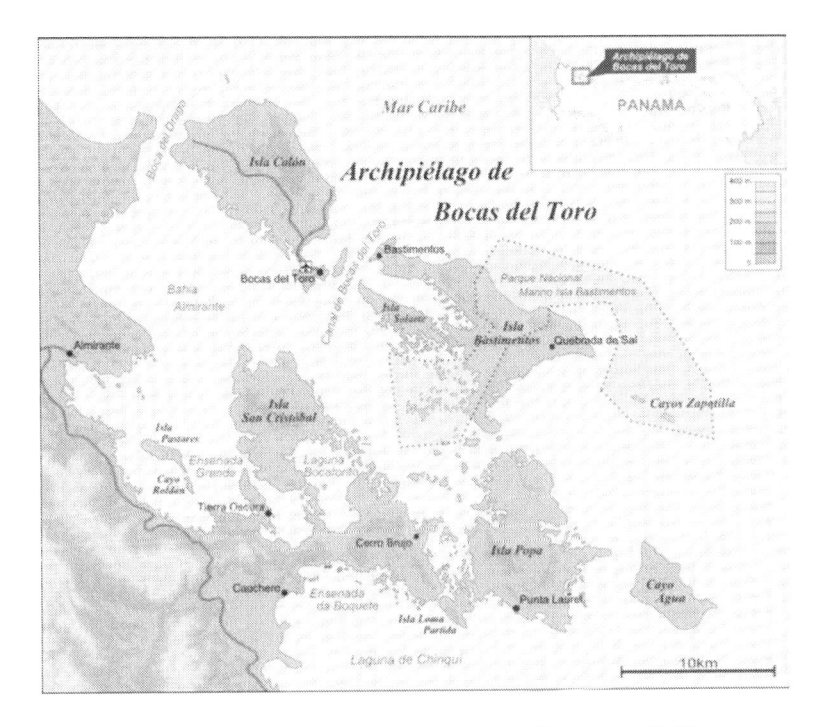

A Visit to a Forgotten Part of the Caribbean

I've always been drawn to out-of-the-way places than the obvious destinations. I certainly discovered one when I visited the obscure islands of Bocas del Toro in Panama.

I'd never ever heard of the archipelago until I met a retired doctor at last year's Auction Napa Valley. A true Cajun, Dr. Rita Rae lives part time in Lake Charles, Louisiana, and part in Bocas, as it's called there.

Early in January, she was reading my *Insider's Guide to Napa Valley* – you tend to read a lot when you're in Bocas – and rekindled the friendship by email.

I guess I was ready for a tropical adventure, for when she invited me to visit, I quickly checked my schedule, frequent flyer miles and found I could slip away.

I'd never been to Central America, but I've spent a lot of time in the eastern Caribbean and some in Cozumel.

Panama is due south of Miami, so I flew through Houston on United Airlines, almost a direct route. I saw flights for about $600 round trip, too.

Unfortunately, connections were bad, so I ended up spending a night in Panama City, a surprisingly, big, progressive and modern city filled with skyscrapers and many more being built. They're even finishing up a subway, though for now, traffic is challenging.

You fly into the international airport, but depart for Bocas on Air Panama at a former U.S. air base right by the impressive Panama Canal, which is about open a major expansion.

The flight to Bocas left at 6:30 a.m. The two others mid afternoon and in the evening don't mesh with flights from San Francisco.

A bit about Bocas
People have many misconceptions about Panama. In the first place, the S-shaped country lies east-west, not north-south. The capital Panama City, is on the Pacific side and most of the northern (not eastern) shore is rain forest or jungle, and no roads extend along it (or to the far eastern part next to Columbia).

You can drive along the more hospitable Pacific coast and take a winding mountain road over the continental divide, which tops 11,000 feet at places, to a town near Bocas and catch a ferry, but the bus takes 11 hours, fine for poor young backpackers but not me.

The 1-hour flight was uneventful if expensive. Below us was nothing but greenery and lakes. No roads, no towns, nothing manmade. Soon we dropped toward the sea.

A sea of islands

The Bocas del Toro archipelago, like some other parts of the Caribbean coast of Central America, is home to a colony of Afro-Caribbeans brought from Jamaica to work on the banana and other fruit plantations in the early 1900s. They speak a sing-song English patois with many archaic and local words, and can be challenging to understand but most can also speak regular English, too.

Of course, as part of Panama, the government and many people speak Spanish, too. Most of the groceries and many other businesses are owned by Chinese-Panamanians. Many native people live here, too.

The area is out of the hurricane belt, but does get some big storms, and mosquitoes and sand fleas demand you use Off! insect repellant. I wasn't bothered, but Rita Rae was. I guess I'm old and tough.

Bocas town itself lies on a peninsula on Isla Colón. The northern part faces the Caribbean, but the bay side is placid and many islands lie a short boat ride away. Some have inhabitants, including Bastimentos with a national park and an old-time Afro-Caribbean village.

Bocas town was created in the early 1900s by the United Fruit Company, which virtually governed most of Central America at one time.

The company built typical small Caribbean homes for workers and some businesses, but abandoned the area after a blight hit the bananas and the workers unionized. The buildings are mostly wood in bright and pastel colors, many exhibiting traditional gingerbread.

The town is slightly shabby, as tropical places tend to be, but charming and friendly. It's been discovered mostly by backpackers and other low-end travelers, many from Europe, and none of the hotels are big or fancy, just traditional Caribbean guest houses, beach resorts, informal hotels and hostels.

Some don't even have air-conditioning, just fans – and mosquito nets – but the seat breezes tend to keep it comfortable out of the sun.

But you can get a clean room for $18, for $25 with a private bath and air-conditioning. They use U.S. money, though they also have local coins and Balboa coins equal to $1.

A few newer places built by Israelis and Dutch are a bit nicer, but similar.

However, I was staying in Dr. Rita Rae's guest room.

She picked me up at the tiny airport right in town with Bill, who manages her property when she's gone and lives on the first floor. He also served as her driver.

The road to Rita Rae's

After a breakfast at one of the small new hotels on a patio over the water, we headed for her home. We were driving along a decent road out of town along the Caribbean when suddenly the pavement ended and we were on the beach.

The road is simply a path with huge holes full of seawater, a few coconuts and even a coconut tree trunk or two on the way. Needless to say, her vehicle is a truck.

After a long third of a mile, we turned into Rita Rae's lovely home set back from the beach almost facing the Caribbean.

The living quarters is on the second floor partly surrounded by a deck with Bill's room and other space below. It's very modern inside with top appliances, Wi-Fi, satellite TV, you name it.

Touring and eating

After I got a tour of the property including the pool, and settling in, we headed out to explore town. Soon we found a panga, the local boats with huge outboard engines, for the short trip over to the next island, Carenero, which contains a few casual resorts and beach restaurants. I think it cost $1.

There, we enjoyed a delicious lunch at Gigi's built on piers over the water. I had a Margarita, which was $5 and obviously made from fresh limes.

I also had ceviche of fresh fish and a delicious mahi-mahi (dorado) sandwich. It was $8. A local beer was $1.50. I could have gotten a Chilean wine for $3, all typical prices.

The food was universally delicious, for virtually everything I ordered was fresh seafood, which was served with simply prepared vegetables and salad. The fruit was excellent, too.

The only fish commonly caught there were mahi-mahi and tuna, but they get shrimp and other fin fish from the cooler Pacific side.

From there, we wandered along the beach to the next bar on a pier, the Pickled Parrot, and spent some time catching up and talking to the bartender and other patrons including some young Israelis just out of the army.

Then we caught a boat picking up empty beer bottles – they reuse them – back to town, did some shopping – there's not much upscale merchandise or art even – and eventually headed back to the house.

Rita Raw and me on Rip Tide

We got off at a typical seedy Caribbean beach bar in an abandoned boat called the Rip Tide filled with fellow expatriates and friends.

The Louisiana Saints team was playing in the football playoffs, however, so we headed back so Rita Rae could watch that.

That night, a Friday, we came into town again, and ate at second-story Lemongrass over the water. Service was slow but the southeastern Asian food was good,. A band played old Cuban music, which I love, and a French-Canadian fiddle player joined in.

The music in Bocas seemed caught in a time warp, and that's hardly surprising since many of the musicians are expatriates from the states who drifted down long ago.

Later, we went to Lili's Café, where many musicians were joining in a jam session and the Grateful Dead-era fans loved it.

Many of the locals are older, some gainfully retired expatriates like Rita Rae, others the flotsam and jetsam you find all over the tropics. Many younger people were visiting, but most ended up in other bars.

Around 11:30 p.m., we left, and as Bill wasn't around, we had a little trouble finding a taxi, but eventually made it home.

The next day, Sunday, was beach day.

Bill drove us farther out the so-called road, which turned inland a bit and became a decent unpaved road. At the end was Bluff Beach, a hangout for surfers. It directly faces the Caribbean, and the seas build up for 1,000 miles to get there. I didn't go swimming.

It also had a little beach bar for more beers and tropical drinks, and I pretended to read while I gazed at the roaring surf and young beach bunnies. We also enjoyed tasty tacos from langusta, the local clawless lobsters.

After that, we wandered over to a nearby open-air restaurant featuring lively music; Rita Rae seemed to know half the patrons.

The Margarita was so good that I had another for dessert, as they say, and I enjoyed a real treat:

Suddenly the skies opened up like we were at the bottom of Niagara Falls. The rain drowned out the band and talking, and beachgoers nearby were soaked before they could run for cover.

Rita Rae was a gracious hostess, and she took Bill and his local girlfriend and me to the Bocas Wine Bar, a surprisingly good restaurant, for dinner.

I almost drank the delicious coconut sauce on the prawns. Bill didn't drink, fortunate since we were caught in a checkpoint on the way home. It's one way the local government makes money from tourists.

More exploring
The next day, I wanted to explore town more, which we did, but also relaxed on the patio of a guest house Rita Rae stayed in while she was building her house, which is one of the largest on the island.

Lunch was more fish plus coconut rice at Lili's while Rita Rae enjoyed Killin' Me Man Chicken Salad.

I should mention that hot sauce made from Scotch Bonnet pepper was on every table, and widely used, delicious but incendiary.

We had a fine but reasonable dinner at El Pecado run by a French-Canadian and I splurged on some real Chablis, though it wasn't expensive by Napa standards.

I also had some ceviche, and I fear it might have contributed to a rough night and next morning, when we had planned a trip to another island. I skipped that and lunch, hanging close to my bathroom.

They took me to the airport midafternoon, and I started feeling better by the hour. I was able to eat part of a gyro at a modest Greek place across from my room in the new Veneto Casino Hotel, then catch the flight home the next day at 10 a.m., arriving in San Francisco at 6 p.m. after losing three hours.

It was good to see another corner of the Caribbean, and see how much it had in common with the less-developed islands of the Antilles.

I look at the map and see the Bay Islands of Honduras, the Columbian islands of San Andres and Providencia way out in the Caribbean Sea, and Isla Mujeres and Isla Holbox off Yucatan, and I can't help wondering what they're like, too. Maybe they're my next tropical adventure.

The Caribbean Cuisine

Few cuisines sound better than Caribbean food. West Indian ingredients — exotic fruits and vegetables and fresh seafood — sound exciting and the combinations innovative. In practice, however, food in most Caribbean islands rarely tastes as good as it sounds.

This is especially true on the English- and Dutch-speaking islands, which inherited a bland culinary tradition from their colonial masters that even local spices can't overcome.

No one has ever gone to an English island for the food.

This isn't true on the French islands, of course. They've inherited the best traditions of French cooking and enhanced it with local ingredients.

One popular tourist destination, Antigua, illustrates the problem. Revolting against slavery that ended more than 150 years ago, the local people don't like to work in fields or to serve other people, especially those they consider wealthy white tourists.

The island is as dry as California without the technology, inclination or funds to adopt modern techniques of agriculture. As a result, local produce is scarce and uninspiring. And like its neighbors, Antigua's attitude defines the term insular. Each island is a different country or political jurisdiction that erects greater barriers to the products of fellow islands than to those from North America.

As a result, the most common food on Antigua is chicken imported from Georgia or Arkansas.

Goats and sheep abound, but appear on the tourist table less than imported beef. Finding fresh fish often requires a trip to the dock early in the morning, and it's sometime difficult to locate fresh fruit, even in season.

Tourists, of course, typically don't really want to try such local delicacies as bull foot soup or fried breadfruit anyway, so they get hamburgers, barbecued chicken, French fries and the occasional overcooked lobster.

If they do go to local restaurants, the local food sometimes seems to be overcooked animal parts and unidentifiable vegetables in spicy grayish-brown sauce, often containing gummy dumplings. Almost everything else seems fried. And many dishes are eaten drenched in hot sauce.

Nevertheless, it is possible to find excellent West Indian food. More to the point, it's possible to produce better-than-traditional Caribbean dishes, just as new American Greek cooking eschews the vast quantities of oil used at home.

The following are authentic recipes, lightened in some cases, but typical of the best food available. Aside from the fritters, tasty enough to justify the frying, none are fried. Each recipe serves six people unless otherwise stated.

Island Ingredients

Most Caribbean food ingredients are reasonably available in U.S. supermarkets, partly because of the influx of Caribbean and Latin American immigrants. Some are found primarily at specialized markets.

At any rate, they're common in California, sometimes under alternate names. Western Caribbeans call dasheen or taro leaves callaloo, for example, but Easterners use the name for Chinese spinach (yin choi), sold in the U.S. as New Zealand spinach.

Suitable substitutes include kale, chard, or spinach.

Many of the ingredients are indigenous to the area, though others were brought by African slaves or colonists. The infamous Captain Bligh imported breadfruit from Tahiti as a humanitarian gesture to feed the slaves, for example.

The most popular fruits are bananas, mangos, papayas (paw-paws), guavas, pineapples, limes and coconuts. They're cooked as well as eaten raw or in rum-laced drinks.

Common starchy vegetables include the ubiquitous potato plus other roots and tubers prepared in the same ways: cassava (yuca), dasheen (taro), eddo, yams (hard white or yellow roots, not Louisiana red-orange sweet potatoes) and sweet potatoes.

Breadfruit, plantains (vegetable bananas) and pumpkin (a hard squash) are fruits, but are prepared the same ways as the roots: baked, fried, boiled, scalloped or in salads and soups. Most become starchy if mashed and resemble library paste. Rice is widely eaten, too.

Other popular vegetables include okra, christophene (chayote), dried beans (pigeon, black-eyed, red, pink or black), carrots, corn and cabbage.

Foods are flavored with coconut milk (liquid extracted from shredded coconut), lime, ginger and the inevitable peppers and hot sauces, some truly incendiary. Of course, the Caribbean is famous for spices, especially cinnamon, allspice, mace, nutmeg and cloves.

A variety of seafood inhabits local waters including fish from tiny minnows to dolphin fish (mahimahi or dorado) and huge marlin that are fished commercially.

Conch [conk], the meat of the huge whelk that symbolizes the Caribbean, is popular, but becoming rare because of demand.

One favorite treat of locals is salted cod fish, often with a fruit called ackee that looks and tastes like scrambled eggs.

Though chicken is the most common meat, lamb, pork and beef are popular. Most are imported from the United States. You won't see many sheep on the islands, just lots of goats, but since Americans don't eat goat, many restaurants call the goat meat lamb or mutton. The local meats products are often tough, suitable only for slow cooking methods unless they've been tenderized by marinating in papaya, a natural tenderizer, limes or other acids.

Appetizers and Snacks

Conch Fritters

Fritters filled with various ingredients—animal, seafood, vegetable or fruit —are popular snacks in the Caribbean. Some utilize potatoes or other starches as binders, but most use flour. Conch is traditional, but other possibilities are clams, abalone, whelk (scungilli), shrimp and crab.

Filling
1 pound conch
1 small onion, diced
1 small hot pepper, seeded and diced
Oil to fry

Batter
2 cups flour
1 teaspoon baking powder
1 teaspoon paprika
Salt and pepper
1 beaten egg
Water to mix (about 3/4 cup)

If the conch is fresh, pound it until it's tender; it's as tough as abalone. Grind into small pieces and mix with the onion and pepper, then add the other ingredients, mixing thoroughly. Let the batter sit for a few minutes and drop by large spoonfuls into 1/2 inch of hot oil. Flatten with a spatula and turn to brown on both sides. Drain and serve warm with lime juice, tartar sauce or cocktail sauce. Yields about 25 fritters.

Codfish balls

Fritters featuring dried salt cod (bacalao in Spanish) are popular in many places. These are made with potatoes, but don't contain any peppers so they aren't hot; they're best dipped in a hot sauce.
1/2 pound dried salt cod (weight after removing skin and bones)
2 large peeled and boiled baking potatoes (russets)
1/2 chopped onion
1 lightly beaten egg
pepper -- no salt needed!
oil for deep frying
hot sauce

Soak the fish for at least a few hours, changing water at least once. Flake with a fork or fingers. Mix ingredients and puree in food processor or blender. Shape into small balls using a large melon balled or spoons, then fry until golden. Serve with sauce for dipping.

Akkras
These spicy fritters are composed primarily of black-eyed peas. They suggest the falafel of the Middle East.

2 cups uncooked black-eyed peas
1 seeded and diced green or red bell peppers (or 1/2 of each)
1 small seeded and diced Scotch bonnet or Habanero peppers (be careful!)
3 garlic cloves (not traditional, but adds considerably to flavor)
Salt and black pepper
Oil for deep frying (or less for cooking patties)

Soak the peas in water overnight. Remove skins if you wish, then drain and soak again for a few hours. Drain and combine with peppers, garlic and pepper, then puree in a blender until smooth. Add salt and black pepper. Drop tablespoons of batter in hot oil and fry until golden (You can also shape into patties and cook in 1/4 inch of oil). Drain and serve as an appetizer with hot sauce. Makes 25 fritters

Fried Green Plantains
These twice-fried treats are called tostones in Puerto Rico. They're like fat potato chips and are

pretty bland so are often used with dips or drizzled with garlic oil.

1 large green plantain
Oil for frying
Salt and pepper

Peel and slice the plantain diagonally into ¾-in. pieces. Soak in cold salted water for 30 minutes and dry with towels. Heat about 1/2-in. of vegetable oil in a heavy frying pan over medium high heat, then fry the slices for 2 minutes on each side. Then lower the heat to medium and cook for 5 minutes more, turning slices often but don't let them get too dark. Remove the slices from pan, then flatten to half the original thickness. Return the heat to high and fry the flattened slices until golden on both sides. Remove and drain, then salt and pepper.

Rotis

Rotis, the burritos or wraps of the Caribbean, have East Indian antecedents, but they've become *the* regional fast food. Simply a white flour pancake wrapped around a curried meat or vegetable filling, they've available everywhere at reasonable cost. You can make them hot or mild. This is a mild lamb version.

2 pounds cubed boneless lamb shoulder or leg
flour for dusting lamb
2 tablespoons curry powder (commercial powder is used in the Caribbean)
1 large chopped onion
3 large cloves garlic
2 tablespoons vegetable oil
2 small boiling potatoes, peeled and cubed

2 medium carrots, scraped and sliced
Salt and pepper to taste
Raisins (optional)
Dash hot sauce
1 cup water
Roti bread (large flour tortillas can substitute) and chutney (see recipes below)

    Shake lamb with flour, then brown. Add onion, garlic and curry and sauté until onions are translucent. Add water and bring to boil, then reduce heat, cover and simmer for 20 minutes. Add potatoes and carrots and cook for 20 minutes or until the meat and potatoes are tender. Add raisins and hot sauce if desired.
    When ready to prepare rotis, put scoop of filling in center of 8-inch roti bread (see recipe below), adding chutney, and fold up like a burrito.

Salad and Soups

Avocado and Papaya Salad

Avocados are a popular ingredient in elegant Caribbean dishes, especially salads. This salad combines its richness with sweet papaya and tart lime.

3 ripe avocados
1 large ripe papaya
5 Caribbean or Key limes
4 tablespoons vegetable oil
Salt and pepper to taste
sugar if using North American limes

Peel the avocados and papaya (or carefully remove the flesh), slice them in half. Removing the stone from the avocado and scoop out the papaya seeds. Slice fruit into 1/4-inch slices (the avocado lengthwise, the papaya across) and fan alternate slices on four salad plates. Separately, squeeze two limes and whisk the juice with the oil. Taste; it may be too acid since our limes are sold unripe. Those in the Caribbean are ripe, hence sweeter -- and yellow rather than green. Add a little sugar in necessary. Pour over the salads and garnish each with lime wedges.

Conch Chowder

Caribbeans love spicy hot soups and stews, which they regard as cooling because they make you perspire. There are as many variations of conch chowder as there are conch cooks. As with clam chowders, most spicy red with tomato like this version. A New England clam chowder recipe would serve for a creamy white chowder. You can sometimes find canned or frozen conch; whelk (scungilli) is similar, as is abalone, available canned from Mexico.

2 tablespoons butter
1 onion, peeled and diced
1 clove garlic
1 green bell pepper, seeded and diced
1 whole small hot pepper
2 pints fish stock (or two bottles clam juice plus 1 pint water)
1 lb. peeled and cubed boiling potatoes
1/2-teaspoon chopped dried oregano or thyme leaves
1 can (14 oz) peeled tomatoes, chopped coarsely
1 tablespoon arrowroot in 1/4-cup cold dry white wine
1 lb. pounded and/or ground conch meat
Salt and pepper to taste

Sauté the onions, garlic, and peppers until the onion is translucent. Add stock, potatoes, oregano, and chopped tomatoes and simmer until the potatoes are done. Add conch. Remove the hot pepper. Remove soup from heat and add arrowroot in wine (or water), stirring until the chowder thickens slightly. Serve with hot sauce and johnnycake (see below).

Pumpkin Soup
Caribbean pumpkin is a large spherical squash with sweet orange flesh like Hubbard squash. This soup is offered at both modest stands and expensive restaurants throughout the Antilles.

3 tablespoon butter
1 large onion peeled and chopped
2 cloves garlic peeled and minced
1/4-teaspoon ground ginger
1/4-teaspoon ground cinnamon
1/2-teaspoon turmeric

2 lbs. fresh pumpkin or winter squash, peeled, seeded and cut into cubes
2 potatoes peeled and cubed
2 carrots peeled and sliced
1 pint chicken stock
1/2-pint cream

Sauté the onions and garlic until onions are translucent, then add spices and cook for a minute. Add pumpkin, potatoes and carrots along with the stock, then simmer until the vegetables are soft. Purée in a food processor, then add the cream and serve. Garnish with thin slice of lime or parsley.

Callaloo Soup
Callaloo is the name of both a leafy green and a spicy soup. As with many classic dishes, variations abound, some containing crab or okra.

2 lb. callaloo (see ingredients at end of page), chard or kale, washed
1 large ham hock or 1 lb. meaty bacon or salt pork
1 large onion, peeled and sliced
1 garlic clove, minced
1 teaspoon dried thyme
1 small fresh hot pepper
juice of two small limes
2 pints chicken stock

First plunge the greens in boiling water for a minute, then cool rapidly in cold water to set the bright green color. Chop coarsely and set aside. Then bring the meat to a boil in a large amount of water, then soak for an hour and drain to remove excess saltiness. Chop the meat finely and heat in heavy pan to render fat. Discard all but one tablespoon of fat.

Sauté onions, garlic, pepper and thyme until the onion is translucent, then add the greens. Add stock and simmer for half an hour. Remove hot pepper, add lime juice and puree until smooth, then serve with hot sauce. Garnish with sour cream or yogurt.

Seafood

Caribbean Grilled Fish

Excellent-tasting fish inhabit the Caribbean. Steaks from firm-fleshed fish like dorado (mahi-mahi) and wahoo (a type of mackerel) are popular grilled.

Six 3/4-in. thick fish steaks
Juice from three limes plus 3 limes for garnish and taste
Vegetable oil
Salt and pepper

Brush the fish on both sides with lime juice, then oil. Place over hot charcoal fire and cook for about five minutes, then turn once and finish cooking five minutes. Serve immediately with lime slices.

Red Snapper Creole

Creole sauces of tomato, onion, sweet and hot peppers, celery and garlic sautéed in oil are popular on seafood, poultry and vegetables from Trinidad to New Orleans. Only the proportions — and the amount of hot peppers — varies. This sauce can be used with other fish, but red snapper fillets are popular.

Six 6-oz. red snapper fillets

Sauce
1/4-cup olive oil

2 ribs celery, sliced crosswise into narrow pieces
1 green bell pepper, halved, seeded and sliced lengthwise into narrow strips
1 red green pepper, ditto
1 small hot pepper, seeded and finely diced
1 large onion, peeled and sliced
4 cloves garlic, peeled and sliced thinly
1/2-teaspoon dried thyme leaves
1 14-oz. can tomatoes (or equivalent in ripe tomatoes)
1/2-cup white wine
1 teaspoon arrowroot in water or wine (optional)
Dash hot sauce
Salt and pepper to taste
Limes to garnish

Sauté the celery and peppers in oil for 3 minutes, then add onions and garlic and stir until onions are translucent. Add thyme, tomatoes and wine and simmer for 20 minutes. The mixture should remain liquid; if necessary, add water. Add fish fillets and poach for ten minutes. Arrowroot in water can be added to thicken the sauce. Serve with lime wedges and hot sauce —islanders use vast amounts.

Antillean Lobster with Garlic-Lime Sauce

Caribbean lobsters are large crawfish that don't have the large edible claws of New England versions. They aren't as rich as New England lobsters, but are so big that one person is usually served half a tail.

In the islands, they're often boiled and frozen, then grilled, guaranteeing a dry, tough meal. And grilling a fresh lobster usually means the outside is dry and burned while the inside remains underdone.

It may be heresy to say so, but grilling looks great, usually tastes bad. Likewise, grilling garlic butter and lime usually gives a burned flavor. Here's a way to avoid those problems with a fresh lobster.

3 live Caribbean lobsters or frozen uncooked lobster tails
Vegetable oil for basting
Juice of three limes
3 garlic cloves, minced
1 stick (4 oz.) butter
Quartered limes for garnish

 Chop lobster in half with cleaver (if frozen, defrost in refrigerator then bring to room temperature just before cooking). Baste with oil only, then place shell side down on grill. Cook 7 minutes, then baste again with the oil, turn and grill only 3 minutes on the cut side to give grilled flavor without burning. Remove from fire and dabble with sauce. Add lime slices for garnish and flavor.
 An alternate is to simply poach the lobster tail (meat side up) in water and white wine or defrost a frozen tail, then drain and serve with the sauce. You can throw it on the grill for a few seconds if you like brown stripes on the lobster, but coat first with oil to keep it from drying out.

Sauce
 Melt butter and add garlic. Simmer for 10 minutes then add lime juice.

Poultry and Meat

Jerk chicken
 Jerking is a barbecue using a spicy hot rubbing paste perfected in Jamaica. Jerk pork is most common, but the technique is used for other meats

and chicken. The most distinctive flavor is of Jamaica pimento (allspice), which is used in the fire in Jamaica. We have to be content with adding it to the rub. There are dozens of jerks, all containing allspice and hot peppers. Most jerk rubs contain many other spices and ingredients.

2 frying chickens, cut into eight parts
Vegetable oil
Jerk rub (below)

Shake chicken pieces with jerk sauce in paper bag. Place chicken over medium low heat on covered grill, preferably over pimento wood or charcoal containing pimento berries soaked in water. Cook for 30 minutes, turning every few minutes. Check by piecing thigh with a knife to ensure juices run clear.

Jerk rub

The most authentic jerk sauce is a dry paste or powder that is rubbed into the meat. Since it doesn't contain sugar, it doesn't burn like tomato-based sauces and is used during the whole cooking process.

1 tablespoon onion powder
2 tablespoons ground allspice (Jamaican pimento)
2 tablespoons cayenne pepper
1 tablespoon salt
1-teaspoon black pepper
1/2 teaspoon ground cinnamon
1/4-teaspoon ground clover
A few grinds of nutmeg

Combine ingredients thoroughly. You can add neutral oil to make a paste if you prefer but it doesn't seem to work well on chicken.

Jerk Pork

Jerk paste

Based on recipe for jerk rub above, you can use fresh onion, preferably green onions and Scotch bonnet peppers, and add to whirring blender. Process into uniform puree. This creates a thick paste, but it doesn't seem to stick well to chicken. For pork, cook long and slowly.

Starchy Vegetables

Baked plantain

Plantains look like bananas on steroids. There are many varieties, and it's worth asking the supplier to make sure what you're buying. The green (unripe) versions are cooked for their starchy filling quality, the ripe ones often fried.

3 large green plantains
2 tablespoons butter
Salt and pepper to taste

Peel plantains, slice in half vertically and lay in small baking dish. Dot with butter, cover and bake for 30 minutes in a 375 degree oven.

Breadfruit gratin

Breadfruit was brought to the Caribbean by the infamous Captain Blight to feed slaves cheaply. It looks like a big grapefruit with bad skin, but when cooked, is like a slightly sweet new potato and can be used in many of the same recipes.

1 medium breadfruit (about 2 lbs.)
3 tablespoons butter

2 garlic cloves, minced
1/2-cup cream
1/2-cup grated mellow cheese
1/2-cup chicken stock or water

Peel and core the breadfruit, then slice 1/4-inch thick. Bring to boil in water, then simmer for five minutes. Drain and discard water. Arrange breadfruit slices in a buttered casserole dish, then dot with butter and pour on mixture of cream, garlic and stock. Sprinkle with salt, pepper and cheese. Cover and bake for 15 minutes in 375 degree oven, then uncover and bake 15 minutes or until breadfruit is done and cheese crusty.

Rice and peas

The Caribbean has hundreds of recipes that feature rice with various types of dried beans, generally called peas in the Caribbean. This is a basic version.

1 ham hock
1 tablespoon cooking oil
1 large onion, chopped
4 garlic cloves, diced
1 rib celery, sliced thinly
1 small fresh pepper, de-seeded and minced
1 carrot, chopped finely
2 springs thyme
2 bay leaves
1 lb. dried beans (red, black, black-eyed, pigeon or pink)
1 quart water
Salt and pepper
2 cups uncooked rice

2 tablespoons coconut oil or butter
Salt and pepper
Chopped green onions
Hot sauce

    If the beans are from the Caribbean, pick over carefully for stones. Soak the beans overnight or bring to a boil for a minute or two, then remove from heat and soak an hour.
    Discard the water (A loss of flavor, but this allegedly removes most of the gas-producing long sugars.) Add vegetable oil to a large pan, then sweat oil from the ham hock for 10 minutes. Add onions, garlic, pepper and carrot and cook until soft. Add beans and herbs and stir, then add water.
    Bring to boil, cover, then reduce heat and simmer for 2 hours or until beans are thoroughly cooked, some mushy. Check often to ensure beans don't dry. If so add more liquid. Add salt and pepper. Separate meat from hock and return to beans.
    Place rice with salt and coconut oil in heavy pan with tight lid. Add 4 cups water and bring to a boil, reduce heat to low and let cook unopened 20 minutes. Then check, cooking 5 minutes more if necessary, and fluff.
    Offer rice and beans in separate dishes. Let each person take a pile of rice and put the wet beans on top. Garnish with chopped green onions and provide hot sauce for flavoring.

Vegetables

Eggplant Creole
    Eggplants, often called aubergine or melongene, are found in many forms in the Caribbean, and eaten

in many ways. This dish is similar to Mediterranean ratatouille.
1/4-cup vegetable oil (olive oil tastes best, but isn't typical of the Caribbean)
1 large eggplant (or two or three small ones)
1 large onion
4 cloves garlic
1 sweet red pepper
1 sweet green pepper
1 fresh hot pepper
2 sprigs fresh thyme
1 can tomatoes
1/4-cup plain vinegar
Salt and pepper to taste

Caribbean eggplants are bitter, so leach out the bitterness by slicing them, then sprinkling with salt and draining for 20 minutes. Then rinse and dry. Sauté the eggplant slices in hot oil until soft, then set aside to make the sauce. Heat oil, then add onion, garlic and peppers. Cook until the onions are translucent, then add thyme, tomatoes and vinegar. Cook until sauce thickens slightly, then pour over eggplant slices in a oven-proof dish and bake for 15 minutes at 375 degrees.

Stuffed christophene
Christophene is the local name for the chayote. This delicate squash can be steamed and served with butter and lime, served au gratin, or stuffed as here.
3 medium christophenes (chayotes)
1 cup dry bread crumbs
1 small onion, chopped finely
2 cloves garlic, minced
3 tablespoons butter
1/4-teaspoon cinnamon

A few grinds of nutmeg
Salt and pepper
Lime wedges

    Sauté onion and garlic in butter until soft, then add spices and crumbs and cook for until well integrated. Slice christophenes in half lengthwise, discarding the seeds. Arrange them cut side up in a shallow baking dish containing 1/2 inch of water.
    Place one-sixth of the filling mixture in each cavity and bake at 375 degrees until the vegetable is soft and the bread crumb mixture crisp. Serve with lime wedges.

Breads

Roti bread

Roti bread looks like flour tortillas, which make fine rotis. This version is more traditional.

1-1/2-cups flour
1-1/2-teaspoons baking powder
1/2-teaspoon salt
1-1/2-tablespoons lard (or other solid fat, but lard works best)
A few tablespoons water

Mix the dry ingredients thoroughly, then work in lard and add enough water to make a soft but not sticky dough. Cover and let rise for an hour. Divide dough into six pieces, then roll out to 8-inch circles and cook individually in a heavy ungreased but well seasoned cast iron or nonstick skillet for about two minutes on each side. They should just start to brown.

Johnnycake

Johnnycake is fried bread dough, an unsweetened flat doughnut hole. Many contain cornmeal for a nutty taste, but they can be made with only white flour. The same dough can be used for dumplings cooked in soups and stews. It's lighter than many local dumplings, which contain no leavening.

1-cup flour
1/2-cup cornmeal
2 teaspoons baking powder
Dash of salt
2 tablespoon butter
A few tablespoons of water
Oil for frying

Mix dry ingredients, then work in butter and add a small amount of water to make a stiff dough. Knead until smooth. Form into small balls 2 inches in diameter, then flatten to 1/2 inch thick. Pour 1/2 inch of vegetable oil in a pan, heat and fry a few cakes at a time, until brown on each side. Serve immediately. They're sodden lumps after sitting for a while.

Sauces

Hot sauce

Each island in the Caribbean has its own commercial and home-made hot sauces. All are nuclear; use them with caution. The strongest are simply peppers (Scotch bonnet, a cousin of the Habanero, is hottest) with vinegar and salt. Some temper the fire with papaya, tomatoes, bell peppers, onion or garlic, and a few, like Tabasco from Louisiana, are fermented and aged for a distinctive flavor.

1 green (not ripe) papaya, peeled, seeded and finely chopped
5 hot peppers, de-seeded and chopped
3 cloves garlic, peeled and minced
1/4 cup fresh lime juice
1/2 cup white vinegar
1 tablespoon hot mustard (for an Antiguan version)
1/4- sweet red bell pepper for highlight color (optional)
Dash of salt

Blend all ingredients but the red pepper into a thick sauce. Add the red pepper and pulse until it's in small flecks. Age for about a week in the refrigerator. Consume with care.

Mango chutney

Chutney, like many other Caribbean standards, originally came from India. A sweet-spicy condiment, it's vital with curries, but also enhances roasted pork, lamb and turkey. Chutney can be made with various fruit, or combinations of fruit, but the most common version uses under-ripe mangoes.

1 green (unripe or slightly ripe) mango peeled, seeded and chopped
1 hot pepper, seeded and diced
1 slice fresh ginger, minced or 1/2-teaspoon ground ginger
1 clove garlic, peeled and minced
2 tablespoons. raisins
3 tablespoons sugar
Juice of small lime
Salt to taste

Combine ingredients and bring to a boil. Reduce heat and simmer for 30 minutes or the mixture thickens. Cool and serve or refrigerate.

Desserts

Flambéed bananas

A classic dessert in the islands is bananas first fried in butter and sugar, then flambéed with rum. It's an festive ending for a Caribbean meal, especially if done at the table.

3 ripe bananas, peeled and sliced lengthwise
1 stick (4 oz.) real butter
3 tablespoons brown sugar or molasses
1/4-cup dark rum — if you use 151 proof Demarara, be careful
Lime wedges (optional)

Melt the butter in a heavy skillet. Add sugar and stir until it melts. Carefully add bananas and simmer for 3 minutes, then carefully turn the bananas. Increase the heat so the mixture bubbles, then add rum and ignite, swishing the skillet to burn the alcohol off. Serve immediately. Some people squeeze on lime juice to balance the sweetness of the dessert.

Pineapple fritters

Antigua grows small pineapples called black pineapples that are unsurpassed anywhere in the world but conventional fruits work well in this recipe, too.

1 pineapple, peeled, cored and sliced into 12 1/4-inch thick rounds
1-1/2-cup self-rising flour (or regular flour plus 1 1/2-teaspoon baking powder)
1/4-cup sugar
1/2-teaspoon salt
1 tablespoon rum

Water for mixing
Oil for frying

Mix the dry ingredients, then add rum and water to make a pancake-like batter. Let sit a few minutes. Dry pineapple slices, then dip in batter and immediately fry in a skillet containing 1/4 inch of oil until brown on each side. Sprinkle with sugar and serve.

Coconut flan
This delicious custard is flavored with shredded coconut and also contains the traditional caramel sauce. It can be made in a large single pie or as individual servings. A nice garnish is toasted fresh coconut.

1 cup sugar
3/4 cup water
2 cups shredded dried coconut (unsweetened is best but hard to find. The packages are slightly larger.)
1 14-oz can of sweetened condensed milk (perhaps use unsweetened with sweetened coconut)
4 lightly beaten eggs
3 tablespoons dark rum
1 1/2 teaspoon real vanilla extract
butter for pan
cinnamon for garnish

Caramelize the sugar by mixing it with water and boiling gently until it's a nice brown color. Use a silver colored pan so you can monitor the color. Don't stir; you can use a brush with water to dissolve the sugar that sticks to the sides of the pan. Be very careful since it can cause a bad burn. Let cool slightly and add 1/4 cup water and stir. Divide caramel among six to eight buttered custard cups or ramekins (Or use a conventional 9 inch Pyrex pie pan) and swirl around so it coats the bottom of the cups.

Separately, combine coconut, milk, eggs, rum and vanilla and mix thoroughly. Divide equally among cups, then bake at 325 degrees in a bain marie (a pan with hot water halfway up the cups) for 30 minutes or until a skewer insert in the middle comes out clean. (Longer, perhaps 45 minutes for the pie pan).

Let cool and invert cups to serve. The caramel sauce will run down the sides of the custards for an attractive presentation.

Based on recipe in *Island Cooking*.

Pineapple cake with pineapple cream sauce

This is a cake similar to a carrot cake with pineapple instead of carrot added. It is served with a rich cream sauce containing pineapple.

2 cups flour
2 teaspoons baking powder
1/4 teaspoon salt
1 cup milk
2 tablespoons butter
4 eggs
2 cups sugar
2 teaspoons pure vanilla extract
1 cup fresh pureed pineapple (or other suitable tropical fruit)

Sift the dry ingredients together and set aside.
Heat the milk and butter.
Beat the eggs, adding sugar until thick and foamy. Add the hot milk and butter mixture and vanilla and mix well. Pour into a previously buttered and floured 11 by 11 inch baking pan. Bake in a 350 degree oven

for about 25 minutes, checking with a skewer to make sure it's done.

Based on recipe for coconut cake in *The New Basics Cookbook*.

Pineapple custard sauce

5 egg yolks
1/4 cup sugar
1/8 teaspoon salt
1 cup cream
1 cup chopped fresh pineapple
1 teaspoon pure vanilla extract
1 teaspoon dark rum

Beat the egg yolks with the sugar aand salt until pale yellow. Mix in the cream, then cook in a double boiler (or very carefully at low heat) stirring constantly. When it gets thick, remove from heat, and stir until cool. Add the chopped pineapple, vanilla and rum. Mix and chill. Serve over cake.

Based on recipe in *Island Cooking*.

Beverages

Rum is *the* drink of the Caribbean. Almost every island makes its own rum or rums — in the case of the French islands, dozens of them. They range from clear to dark and flavorful, and from $2-per-bottle rotgut to libations that rival fine cognacs for after-dinner sipping.

The world's most popular rum by far is Bacardi (pronounced ba car DÍ), which originated in Cuba, but is now made in Puerto Rico, Mexico and elsewhere. The most popular Bacardi rums are light and almost always mixed with strong flavored mixers that would obscure its flavor in any case. Bacardi also makes some excellent darker rums, many of which don't make it to the mainland U.S.

Some are so flavorful that they can be drunk neat, and it's certainly a shame to mix them with strong fruit flavors.

The smaller islands specialize in darker potions, such as Meyer's from Jamaica, Pusser's associated with though not made in the British Virgin Islands and Mount Gay from Barbados.

Cruzan Rum is a product of St. Croix, US. Virgin Islands, where rum has been produced for over two hundred years, though the light version we get on the Mainland isn't the same as that sold there.

All the rums from English- and Spanish-speaking islands are made from molasses, a by-product of sugar production.

The French islands of Martinique and Guadeloupe, on the other hand, make their rums from fresh sugar cane juice.

Think of wine made from fresh grape must versus that made from boiled concentrate and you'll understand why connoisseurs prefer them.

Though most are dark, they have a more delicate aroma and flavor. They're also hard to find and expensive.

Most rum, however, is mixed with Coke, tonic, ginger ale or fruit juices, so light rum is fine. Rum with fruit juice makes the heady punches served to tourists on island excursions by smiling islanders who assure the visitors that the drinks aren't strong, almost surely a fib since the rum is cheaper than the soft drink or fruit mixer!

Beer is the most popular drink with meals. Most islands make their own, and others like Heineken and Red Stripe are brewed on a number of islands.

Some of the local brews are excellent, some mediocre, but most are light and served very cold to complement the hot climate.

Not all the drinks are alcoholic. Many fruits and flavoring are squeezed or seeped to make tasty and refreshing concoctions, some tart, some sweet. They include passion fruit, sorrel flowers (not related to the green herb), lime, mango, tamarind, papaya, pineapple, coconut, guava and soursop (guanábana).

A few commercial soft drinks like Ting, a light grapefruit concoction, are superb and serve wider distribution in the U.S.

Rum punch

Rum punches can be based on any fruit juice. A popular one is made from mixed tropical fruits, with rum added and nutmeg grated over the top. The classic rum punch has more bite. It can be made in any quantity using the traditional ratios.

1 parts sour (fresh lime juice, not that horrible bottled stuff!)
2 parts sweet (sugar syrup or Grenadine [pomegranate syrup])

3 parts strong (rum — in this case, dark rum is justified)
4 parts weak (water, soda water or orange or other light fruit juice).

If the "parts" are ounces, it's 10 ounces total, and is served in a tall glass with ice. Garnish with a lime or other fruit slice and grated nutmeg. Serves one

Daiquiri
The classic Daiquiri becomes frozen if you have a blender. Warning makes a 12-volt version for boats, a necessity in the tropics!
2 oz. light rum
2 oz. fresh lime juice
1 oz. sugar syrup
Crushed ice
Mix ingredients. Blend to a slush for a frozen version. Garnish with lime slice. Serves one.

Piña colada
The name suggests a Spanish origin, but piña coladas are ubiquitous throughout the Caribbean. Though they contain pineapple (piña), the distinctive coconut flavor comes from cream of coconut, thick liquid that rises on coconut milk, the liquid extracted from ripe coconut flesh mixed with water or coconut water (the almost tasteless liquid from ripe coconuts many people confuse with coconut milk).

2 oz. dark rum
4 oz. pineapple juice (or 6 oz. fresh ripe pineapple)
1 oz. coconut cream (sold commercially as Coco Lopez)
Dash of lime for tartness to balance all the sweetness and richness

Lime garnish

Blend the rum, pineapple (juice), coconut cream and lime squeeze with ice in a blender. Garnish with lime. Serves one

Made in the USA
Columbia, SC
20 May 2025